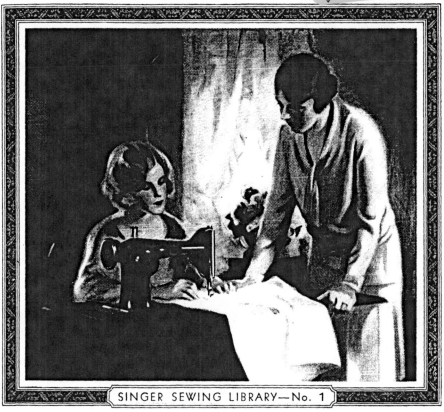

SINGER SEWING LIBRARY—No. 1

SHORT CUTS
TO
HOME SEWING

The Modern Singer Way

PUBLISHED BY

SINGER SEWING MACHINE CO. Inc.

FOREWORD

FOR more than three-quarters of a century the great Singer organization has devoted itself to the solution of women's sewing problems in every country in the world. Out of this daily contact with thousands of home sewers, Singer experts have developed a constant succession of improvements in the machines themselves, numerous ingenious, easy-to-use attachments and many clever short-cut methods which save time and enable you to do more of your own sewing than you ever dreamed would be possible. Most factory machines are Singers, too, and practically all of the charming effects seen on expensive ready-made clothing may be successfully attained at home by Singer methods. They are not difficult or complicated and can easily be applied by the average woman. The object of this book is to show and explain these methods, so that you may be able to develop the full possibilities of your sewing machine in the creation of the many stitched articles so essential to the comfort and pleasure of yourself, your family and your home. Any Singer Shop, which you will find in every city, will be glad to help you by further explanation or personal instruction. There is no charge or obligation for this assistance, which we are pleased to give as a part of Singer Service.

Singer Sewing Machine Company
INCORPORATED

How easy it is today to make one's own clothes

By MARY BROOKS PICKEN
Dressmaking Editor, Pictorial Review

OR twenty years I have been interested in women and their sewing. Ever since I was a very little girl I have loved to sew myself. From doll dresses of the simplest sort to stately gowns—all have held my interest and given me in their creation a great deal of happiness.

WHEN I was a little girl I was taught to thread a Singer Sewing Machine. I was taught the essentials of machine sewing—an even feeding of the material under the presser foot, an easy stop, the necessity of a correct length of stitch, an even tension, the importance of frequent oiling, and of sitting correctly at the machine when I sewed.

YARDS and yards and miles and miles of sewing were done on that treasured old Singer. Even now, it still gives me a little thrill of delight when I sit down before it, worn and scarred though it is, and see the stitches interlocking in the cloth as perfectly as ever.

I USED to sew at night a great deal and even with the treasured old machine would put rugs underneath to prevent the noise from disturbing my father and mother who insisted that there was a bed time and that busy eyes needed resting.

FASHIONS

Last year I had my choice of a gift between a new Singer Electric Machine and a Radio. Of course I took the sewing machine, and it is of my new enjoyment that I want to tell you.

I have loved the old machine and it still gives excellent service. But this new one has been to me like a new toy, as a whole big electric train would be to an eager little boy. It is lifted out on the porch, down in the living room, in the sitting room upstairs—all over the house. The family read to me while I sew. The children tell me of the movie they saw, the program at school. The neighbors come in and visit. And all the while I am sewing away, seam after seam, yards of them, all be-

CUTTING OUT

cause this lovely new machine makes no noise.

The attachments I use with the ease that I do the scissors. A hem is turned or ruffles are formed or pleats are made as simply as a pan of biscuits is browned, merely by using the conveniences that the little box of attachments provides for me.

The motor is as silent as a book, the little light at the back gives perfect lighting no matter in what corner or nook I choose to work, and I find myself piling up exquisite dainties in lingerie, curtains, dresses for mother, aprons for the kitchen, dish towels, laundry bags, so many things that the house has long been needing.

Truly the new Singer machines have made sewing a delight for all

THE PATTERN

of us. When I look back fifteen or twenty years and then consider the conveniences we have today, I realize the more how fortunate we are in the facilities we have for making beautiful clothes for ourselves.

TODAY almost every woman has at least one good fashion magazine. Even though she lives in a village or on a farm far from fashion centers, she knows as soon as her city sisters about the correct styles and she can know what is becoming for her.

So GREAT has been the improvement in the modern pattern, with its printed directions or construction guides, that she can select a design in keeping with fashionable good taste and successfully make it by simply following the directions given.

SINGER SHORT CUTS

TRIMMING

FABRICS grow lovelier every season. So colorful, so soft and lustrous, they are a joy to handle and to use.

BUT most amazing and most satisfying of all is the modern sewing machine itself, without which all other aids would be futile. No matter what type of Singer machine you may choose for your needs, it is so easy to operate, so smooth running, so quiet, so efficient in its quick completion of the sewing you ask it to do that it is a delight to use. The task you once thought tedious becomes a joy. Seams flow like magic. And with the aid of ingenious attachments, the most skillful work can be done more perfectly than by hand and in a mere fraction of the time. Hems, plaits, ruffles, binding, braiding—all those deft details that add to the beauty of the frocks you make, are easily and quickly done because the modern Singer has made them as matter of course as simple seams and stitches.

I AM GLAD this book has been prepared to show you just how simple it is to use these ingenious devices, and how to care for and use your machine to get the very most out of it.

I HOPE you will study it carefully so that you will turn confidently to your sewing machine whenever there is sewing of any kind to be done. The more you use it, the more you will depend upon it. And gradually a sentiment will grow up around it. You will think of your sewing machine as I do of mine, as a never-failing friend, as one who has helped you in the joy of creating lovely things for those you love, and one who has helped to make your home a more treasured place in which to find your happiness.

Mary Brooks Picken

SUCCESS

HOW TO CARE FOR AND OPERATE
YOUR SEWING MACHINE

The Principal Parts of Lock-Stitch Sewing Machines and Their Uses

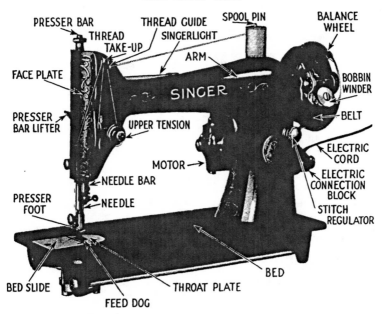

FIG. 1. PRINCIPAL PARTS OF THE HEAD

Head—the part above the table (Fig. 1) containing the stitching mechanism.

Spool Pin—Spindle on which spool rests.

Thread Guide—Supports the thread on its passage from the spool to tension disc.

Arm—the curved part of the head containing the mechanism for driving the needle and handling the upper thread.

Bed—the flat portion of the head, under which is mounted the mechanism for driving the shuttle and handling the lower thread.

Balance Wheel—the wheel at the right of the head driven by the **belt.**

Bobbin Winder—the mechanism for automatically winding bobbins.

Stitch Regulator—the parts which control the length of the stitch.

Upper Tension—the means for controlling the delivery of the upper thread from the spool.

Thread Take-up—the mechanism which pulls up the slack in the thread and locks the stitch.

Needle Bar—the vertical bar to which the **needle** is attached and which carries the upper thread down through the fabric at each stitch.

5

Presser Bar—the vertical bar to which the **presser foot** is attached. This bar is surrounded by a spring which holds the fabric down against the feed dog when sewing but may be released by raising the **presser bar lifter.**

Face Plate—the vertical plate on the left of the arm which may be removed to give access to the needle bar, presser bar and take-up.

Throat Plate—the plate in the bed directly under the needle through which the needle passes and through which the feed dog projects upward.

Feed Dog—the toothed part which projects upward through slots in the throat plate, carrying the fabric from the operator at each stitch. The movement of the feed dog is controlled by the stitch regulator to give the desired length of stitch.

Bed Slide—the flat plate or plates at the left of the bed which may be opened to give access to the shuttle or bobbin case and other parts of the lower stitch forming mechanism.

Bobbin—the metal spool on which thread is wound to furnish the lower or shuttle thread supply.

Shuttle or Bobbin Case—the container in which the bobbin is placed and around which the loop of the needle thread is passed in forming the lock stitch.

Rotary or Oscillating Hook—the part which enters a loop of needle thread and carries it around the bobbin case. In the long bobbin machine (Singer No. 127) this function is performed by the shuttle, which also acts as a bobbin case.

Lower Tension—the spring on the shuttle or bobbin case which controls the delivery of thread from the bobbin.

Motor—the electric motor drives the machine by means of a fabric belt. It is attached by a single screw to the back of the head.

Singerlight—the electric lamp and reflector which throws its rays on the bed of the machine.

Electric Connecting Block—the plug and socket connection which connects the motor and Singerlight with the electric current.

Formation of the Lock Stitch

The lock stitch made by sewing machines consists of an upper or needle thread and an under or bobbin thread locked together in the material which is being stitched, the lock being formed by passing the upper around the lower thread and tightening them together in the middle of the fabric.

Fig. 2. Formation of the Lock Stitch

When a stitch has been completed and before each succeeding stitch is commenced, the fabric being stitched is carried from the needle by the feeding mechanism and upon the length of its movement depends the length of the stitch.

The presser foot holds down the fabric, prevents it from rising with the needle and holds it in contact with the feed dog while the feeding takes place.

6

Wind the Bobbins Evenly

A bobbin must be wound evenly to work properly in the machine. Great care should be taken in winding bobbins to have the thread placed on the bobbin smoothly and evenly, and the bobbin should never be wound so full that it is tight in the bobbin case or shuttle. See Fig. 3. A correctly wound bobbin will insure a smooth-running thread from the shuttle and will prevent an uneven stitch, which may occur if the thread is placed on the bobbin unevenly.

E 4404

FIG. 3. UPPER BOBBIN CORRECTLY WOUND. LOWER BOBBIN INCORRECTLY WOUND

If the thread winds to one side of the bobbin, the guide which carries the thread from the bobbin winder to the bobbin may be bent a trifle, away from the side at which the thread piles up, with a pair of pliers. See Fig. 4. Care should be taken when making an adjustment of the winder not to bend it too far.

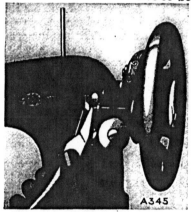

FIG. 4. ADJUSTING THREAD GUIDE

Always make it a point to have a sufficient quantity of bobbins on hand so that it is unnecessary to wind one color of thread on a partly wound bobbin of another color. Bobbins wound in this manner are often uneven, and the ends of the threads become tangled, causing no end of trouble in the bobbin case.

Increasing the Pressure on the Bobbin Winder

If the pressure of the rubber ring against the hub of the balance wheel is not sufficient to wind the bobbin, loosen the adjusting screw (see Fig. 5) and press the bobbin winder lightly until the rubber ring is in contact with the hub of the balance wheel, then tighten the screw. This type of winder is found on Singer 66, 99, 115 and 15-30 machines.

(NOTE: The number of the machine you are using will be found in the instruction book furnished with the machine).

7

If the rubber ring becomes worn or if oil has been allowed to come in contact with the rubber, the ring will not have the proper contact with the wheel and will slip when attempting to wind a bobbin. A worn or oily ring should be replaced.

The bobbin winder on the Singer 66, 99, 101, 115 and 15-30 machines has an automatic stop which releases the winder from the balance wheel when the bobbin has been wound sufficiently full.

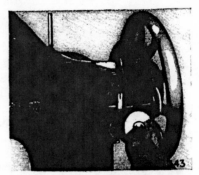

FIG. 5. ADJUSTING PRESSURE ON BOBBIN WINDER

Proper Needle and Thread Important

A perfect stitch can be obtained only when the thread is selected to suit the fabric which is to be stitched and the needle is the correct size for the thread. If the needle is too fine for the thread and the material to be sewn it is quite likely to break when crossing a seam. If a large needle is used on fine material the perforations made by the needle will show on the finished work. A table of correct needles for the various sizes of silk and cotton is given in the instruction book for each machine. This table should be carefully followed when ordering needles and when changing them for various classes of work.

NOTE: Care should be taken to see that only genuine Singer needles are used in Singer machines.

Testing a Needle

An important essential for good work is that the needle be perfectly straight.

A straight needle can be determined by placing the flat side of the needle on the slide plate of the machine or any other perfectly flat solid surface. Hold the needle flat to the plate and the plate up to the light as shown in Fig. 6. A straight needle will show an even amount of light under it and the point will be in line with the shank, while a crooked or bent needle will show closer to the plate or further from it at the point.

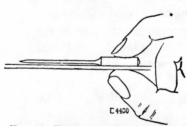

FIG. 6. TESTING A NEEDLE FOR STRAIGHTNESS

8

Setting the Needle Properly

Turn the balance wheel over towards you until the needle bar rises to the highest point. Loosen the thumb screw of the needle clamp, release and remove the old needle. Place the new needle in the needle clamp, making sure that the flat side of the needle is against the needle bar. In other words, have the flat side of the needle to the right. Push the needle up as far as it will go and tighten the clamp. See Fig. 7.

FIG. 7. SETTING THE NEEDLE

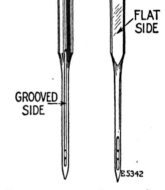

FIG. 8. FLAT AND GROOVED SIDES OF NEEDLE (ENLARGED)

You will note from Fig. 8 that the side of the needle with the flat on the shank has a short groove at the eye while the other side has a long groove. The thread must lie in this long groove when sewing. If the needle is not placed correctly in the machine it will not sew.

The Necessity for Proper Tensions

The tensions on the sewing machine must be adjusted to suit various fabrics. There are two tensions, the upper and the lower. The upper tension controls the thread from the needle, while the lower tension controls the thread from the shuttle or bobbin case.

The definition of the word tension as given in the dictionary is: "stress by pulling." It is the pulling of the threads together that completes a stitch on the sewing machine. After the needle thread passes around the shuttle, the upper thread must be pulled to take up the slack and complete the stitch by locking both threads together. If both are under proper tension, the lock occurs in the center of the material being sewn and a perfect stitch is formed as in Fig. 9.

9

FIG. 9.   BOTH TENSIONS CORRECT

FIG. 10.   TIGHT UPPER TENSION

FIG. 11.   TIGHT LOWER TENSION

If the tension on the needle thread is too tight, or if that on the bobbin thread is too loose, the needle thread will lie along the upper surface of the material as illustrated in Fig. 10.

If the tension on the bobbin thread is too tight, or if that on the needle thread is too loose, the bobbin thread will lie straight along the under side of the material as shown in Fig. 11.

If too tight a tension is used on fine material the threads may break when the material is pressed flat. A bias seam will pucker if the tension is tight. If the tension on a flat seam is too loose there is danger of the thread being pulled out. A long stitch and a loose tension are often used when basting, so that the stitches may easily be pulled from the material.

How to Adjust the Tensions

The tension on the upper thread is regulated by turning the nut E, shown in Fig. 12, to the right to tighten and to the left to loosen.

Tension on the under thread is regulated by the screw which holds the spring under which the thread passes, on the long shuttle or the round bobbin case. Turn this screw to the right to tighten and to the left to loosen. Use the small screw driver for this purpose.

FIG. 12.   ADJUSTING THE UPPER TENSION

If there is difficulty in tightening the under tension there may be a knot of thread caught under the spring on the shuttle or bobbin case. Loosen the tension screw sufficiently, release the knot and remove it.

The tension on the needle thread should be regulated only when the presser bar is down. If you are using the correct thread for the needle the tension may be regulated by adjusting until the thread just barely bends the needle when the thread is pulled through as shown in Fig. 13. The under thread should be adjusted to pull as near like the upper thread as possible. When

FIG. 13.   TESTING UPPER AND LOWER TENSIONS TOGETHER

pulling the under thread care should be taken to see that it is pulling free from the presser foot. (See Fig. 13).

Fine materials require a light tension, while heavy materials require more tension to produce a perfect stitch.

Preparing to Sew

Pull sufficient thread through the needle to start sewing, hold the end of the thread in the left hand and with the right turn the balance wheel over until the needle goes down and the under thread is pulled up through the needle hole in the throat plate. (See Fig. 14). Lay both ends back under the presser foot before starting to sew. This will prevent the under thread from becoming caught in the bobbin case when starting to sew.

FIG. 14. PULLING UP UNDER THREAD

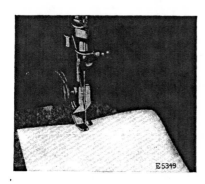

FIG. 15. BEGINNING A SEAM

The edge of the garment to be stitched should be placed just far enough under the presser foot so that the first stitch may be taken in the material. Never place the material so far in front of the needle that the first stitch will not be taken in the material, as this will allow the thread to become caught in the bobbin case; also the material may not feed under the foot properly unless the edge has been caught with the needle. Always lower the presser bar before starting to sew, bringing the tension into operation and preventing the thread from being caught in the bobbin case. See Fig. 15 for the proper starting of material under the presser foot.

Finishing a Seam

When finishing a seam, never sew beyond the end of the material. Stop the machine by placing the hand on the balance wheel shortly before the end of the seam is reached. This will prevent the thread from becoming caught in the bobbin case. See Fig. 16.

Do not attempt to release the material from the machine until the take-up lever is at the highest point. See T, Fig. 20. When the take-up is in this position and the presser foot is raised, the tension is released.

11

Fig. 16. Finishing a Seam

Always take the material from the machine by pulling it straight back away from you.

Always have a sufficient length of thread to prevent its pulling through the needle when you start to sew the next seam. Pull the material back from you far enough to allow the upper and l o w e r threads to enter thread cutter I, Fig. 14. Hold thread with both hands and cut with a quick downward motion.

Hints for Sewing Various Seams

Always keep the material to the left of the presser foot, allowing the seam to extend to the right. This helps to prevent machine oil from soiling the goods and allows greater freedom of feeding than when the garment is allowed to pass under the arm of the machine.

In stitching a skirt, all patterns are made so that the seams must be stitched from top down. This is true of every seam in a garment. In stitching a blouse the shoulder seams must be stitched from neck down, and the under-arm and sleeve seams must be stitched from the armhole down. This is also true when sewing bias seams on a skirt. It must be stitched from the waist line down in order that the pattern will come together correctly.

When sewing a bias edge to a straight edge, place the straight edge against the feed. Hold the bias edge toward you in order to adjust and ease the fullness in to prevent its stretching.

The Cloth Guide

The cloth guide is a part of the sewing machine equipment and is a help in straight stitching. The guide is fastened to the machine by means of the thumb screw as shown in Fig. 17. It can be adjusted to various distances from the needle as desired.

The first practice with the machine after understanding the threading, tensions, etc., is straight stitching. At first use strips of paper without thread

Fig. 17. Cloth Guide

and then sew on muslin, stitching several rows close together. Always use a double piece of material when practicing stitching.

12

Regulating the Length of Stitch

When stitching fine material use a fine needle, fine thread and a short stitch. Heavy material requires a coarse needle and thread and a longer stitch.

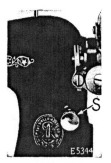

Fig. 18. Stitch Regulating Screw on Singer 66, 99, 127 and 128 Machines

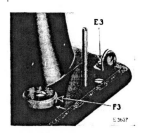

Fig. 19A. Automatic Stitch Regulator on 101 Class Machines

Fig. 19. Stitch Regulating Screw on Singer 15-30 and 115 Machines

The stitch on the 66, 99, 127 and 128 models is regulated by turning screw S, Fig. 18, to the right to lengthen the stitch and to the left to shorten it. The stitch on the 15-30 and 115 models is regulated by screw S, Fig. 19, in a slot on the arm near the bobbin winder. To lengthen the stitch loosen the screw and move downward. To shorten the stitch move the screw upward. When the desired length of stitch is obtained tighten the screw.

About twenty stitches to the inch makes a desirable stitch for ordinary sewing. Sew on a double thickness of muslin, measure off one inch with a ruler and count the stitches.

The 101 Class Machines are equipped with an automatic stitch regulator and the desired length of stitch is instantly obtained by turning a numbered dial to the proper point. (See Fig. 19A, F3.) This can be accomplished while the machine is in operation.

Fig. 20. Regulating the Pressure

Adjusting the Pressure on the Presser Bar

The presser foot rests on the feed dog, holding the cloth in position while sewing. The pressure should be regulated according to the fabric to be stitched, heavy enough to prevent the material from rising with the needle and still enable the work to feed along smoothly. A pressure that is too heavy will cause the machine to run hard and will leave the print of the feed on fine materials.

Increase the pressure by turning the adjusting screw to the right. Lighten the pressure by turning the adjusting screw to the left. (See Fig. 20). The heavier the material the more pressure is required. Fine materials require a light pressure.

13

Cleaning and Oiling

Sewing machines require daily oiling and cleaning if they are used continuously all day. If used moderately, a few hours a day, oiling and cleaning once or twice a week is sufficient. A sewing machine, like all other machinery, will not give proper satisfaction if the working parts are allowed to become dry or gummed with a poor grade of oil. A sewing machine that has not received the proper care will run hard and considerable energy is wasted by using a machine in this condition. Always remove dust, lint, threads, etc., especially in and around the shuttle race, before oiling any part of the machine or stand.

Oiling the Machine Head

The equipment necessary for the proper cleaning of the machine consists of a piece of cheese cloth, a large screw driver, a small screw driver and a stiletto.

Care should be taken to use high-grade machine oil and one drop should be applied to each bearing and each point where there is any friction. It is poor economy to use oil of doubtful quality, as it may gum on the working parts and make necessary a complete overhauling of the machine by a competent repair man.

FIG. 21. CLEANING AND OILING THE HEAD

It is best to be safe and purchase oil from a sewing machine manufacturer interested to have it specially prepared for sewing machines and guaranteed not to gum. Many houshold oils are not suitable for sewing machine use. On Singer machines use only Singer oil.

When planning a thorough oiling, remove the upper thread, slide plate, bobbin. bobbin case, needle and presser foot. Take out the screws in the throat plate (the plate A directly under the presser foot through which the needle passes, Fig. 21) and remove the throat plate. This will enable you to clean and oil the shuttle race. On the 66 and 99 Class machines the oscillating hook is lubricated by oil from a piece of red felt (C, Fig. 21), which touches the top of the hook. This felt wiper should be kept moist at all times.

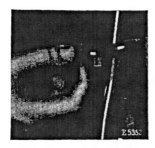

FIG. 22. THE BELT SHIFTER

The face plate should also be removed by taking out screw B (Fig. 21) to give access to the oiling points on the needle bar, presser bar and thread take-up. Put one drop of oil into each oil hole and joint.

On the treadle machines release the belt from the band wheel by turning the lever of the belt shifter, Fig. 22, to the left while the machine is running. To replace the belt after releasing, place the feet on the treadle and start the band wheel in the proper direction. The belt will be thrown on the wheel automatically. Never throw the belt off to the left side of the band wheel, as it is difficult to replace it from this side.

After releasing the belt, turn back the head of the machine in order to reach the oiling points on the under side. By turning the balance wheel slowly you will be able to observe all working parts. Place a single drop of oil at each point, as this is sufficient to lubricate the machine. After oiling all points on the under side, lower the head into sewing position and oil each point on top of the arm. Wipe away all surplus oil, thread up the machine and stitch on a waste piece of material until all surplus oil that might drip onto the goods being sewn has been worked out.

When a machine is used frequently it is not necessary to remove the throat plate, slide, bobbin and bobbin case each time the machine is oiled, but this should be done whenever a thorough cleaning and oiling is required.

To lubricate motor on an electric machine, insert tip of Singer Motor Lubricant tube in tip of both grease cups D (Fig. 21), squeezing a small amount of lubricant in each one. **Never use oil on any part of the motor,** as this causes most of the trouble experienced with small motors.

Oiling the Bobbin Winder

To insure smooth running of the bobbin winder, the oiling points should be observed and care taken to see that they are not neglected when the rest of the machine is oiled. See Fig. 23. If the winder is to be used directly after oiling, do not sit in front of it. If too much oil has been applied it is liable to throw and soil your clothes. Do not allow oil to come in contact with the rubber ring on the bobbin winder, as oil softens the rubber and causes it to slip on the hub of the balance wheel. When this happens, the only remedy is to replace the ring.

FIG. 23. OILING THE BOBBIN WINDER

15

Removing Gummed Oil

If the machine has been idle for several weeks and runs hard, it is probably due to gummed oil. When a machine has become gummed, all working parts should be carefully oiled with kerosene or gasoline. This will loosen the old oil if not too badly gummed. Run the machine rapidly for a few minutes and wipe thoroughly with a piece of cheese cloth. Then oil all working parts with high-grade sewing machine oil. A second oiling after a few hours of use is advisable whenever kerosene or gasoline has been used. If the machine does not run freely after this treatment, it should be examined by a skilled sewing machine adjuster.

COMMON CAUSES OF MACHINE TROUBLES

Causes of Upper Thread Breaking

Machine improperly threaded (see instruction book).
Tensions too tight (see page 9).
Needle bent or having blunt point.
Thread too coarse for size of needle (see instruction book).
Needle too fine for size of thread and material to be sewn (see needle table in instruction book).
Burr on needle hole in throat plate (caused by breaking needle in pulling material from machine).
Burr on needle hole in presser foot (caused from sewing over pins or breaking needle).
Needle set with flat side to outside of clamp (see page 9).
Needle too long for machine, or not all the way up in clamp.
Take-up spring bent or broken. (Send for adjuster to repair).
Tension discs worn so that thread works in groove.

Causes of Lower Thread Breaking

Improper threading of bobbin case or shuttle (see instruction book).
Tension too tight (see page 9).
Thread wound uneven on bobbin or bobbin wound too full (see Fig. 3, page 7).
Spring on bobbin case or shuttle worn to sharp groove.
Burr on under side of throat plate (sometimes caused by sewing over pins or breaking needle).

To Avoid Breaking Needles

Do not sew heavy seams with a needle too fine.

Use proper size of needle for thread and material to be sewn (see needle table in instruction book).

See that the presser foot or attachments are securely fastened to the bar and that the needle goes through the center of the hole.

Do not pull the material to one side when taking it from the machine. The needle may become bent and strike the side of the hole when starting to sew (see page 12).

Do not pull material when sewing. The needle may become bent and strike the back of the needle hole.

Do not bend the needle when pulling out the material before cutting thread (see page 12).

Do not use a needle that is too long. It is liable to come in contact with the bobbin case and break, probably spoiling the case and requiring replacements. (Use only genuine Singer needles in Singer machines).

Do not leave pins in the material after basting and sew over them with the machine.

Skipping Stitches

Needle not accurately set into the needle bar, blunt or bent.

Needle too small for the thread used.

Needle too short for the machine.

Stitches Looping

Looped stitches are usually caused by an improper tension. If the loop is on the **upper** side, it may be corrected by tightening the **under** tension. If the loop occurs on the **under** side, it may usually be corrected by tightening the **upper** tension (see page 10).

See that both the upper and lower threading is correct, that the thread is of good quality and the correct size for the needle.

Test both tensions and stitch on the same material to be sewn.

Looping of stitches is sometimes caused by the placing of the bobbin in the bobbin case or shuttle so that the thread pulls from the wrong side of the bobbin, or by the bobbin being wound too full. (See instruction book).

Machine Not Feeding Properly

Improper feeding is often due to the pressure being too light for the material to be sewn (see page 13).

The feed dog may be worn smooth. This may be determined by running the finger over the teeth. If they are not sharp, the feed dog should be replaced by a competent adjuster.

The stitch regulator may have been turned back so far that the feed is entirely out of action.

Needle may be bent.

Machine Working Heavily

If the machine works hard after standing it is probably gummed and needs a general cleaning (see page 16).

The belt may be too tight and hence putting excessive pressure on the bearings.

When the belt is too loose it slips on the balance wheel and causes the operator to treadle more than is necessary.

Sometimes thread becomes wound around the hub of the balance wheel and the ends of the band wheel crank. With constant running and contact with oil the thread works in next to the bearings so tightly that it makes the machine run heavily. When this happens, remove the thread with a stiletto or other sharp instrument.

Sometimes the bobbin winder snaps down, putting pressure against the balance wheel. Be sure to see that the bobbin winder is released.

Puckered Seams

Tension too tight.

Stitch too long for material being sewn, especially on fine material.

Noisy Treadle

If the treadle is noisy, the screws on which it is pivoted need tightening. Release one of the screws by backing off the nut one or two turns with a wrench, place a screw driver in the slot of the screw and advance the screw toward the treadle just enough to take up the slack. Tighten the nut and test the treadle. If still noisy, repeat the operation on the other side.

THE BINDER AND ITS MANY USES AS
APPLIED TO FAMILY SEWING

Binding Without Basting

Bindings of various materials may be applied with the Binder attachment supplied with Singer Family Sewing Machines. This attachment folds and guides the binding so that, by a simple adjustment, the stitching can be regulated to come close to the edge of the binding.

Binding, when neatly applied, serves as a suitable trimming for wash dresses, children's clothes, underwear, silk or woolen frocks and articles of home decoration. The fashion magazines give endless suggestions for the use of bindings and the ready-to-wear clothes make frequent use of this method of finishing as well as trimming. The following pages give directions for using this time-saving attachment and suggest many ways in which binding may be applied to various curves with perfect results.

Preparing Binding for Use in the Binder

A   E 5065

THE BIAS CUTTING GAUGE

The Bias Gauge is very convenient to use when cutting bias bands from $\frac{7}{16}''$ to $1\frac{3}{8}''$ in width. By placing the gauge on the pointed end of the scissors and setting the blue spring indicator A to the width desired, bias binding may be cut from any material. The letter F is the point to set the indicator for facings, B for binding and C for cording or piping.

The Proper Width of Binding to Use with the Binder

Adjust the blue spring indicator on the Bias Gauge to the letter B and attach to the pointed end of the scissors, as shown in Fig. 24a. Insert the material in the Gauge with the edge even with the indicator and cut as shown in Fig. 24b. Always cut the material on the true bias for use with the Binder.

The binding must measure from $\frac{7}{8}''$ to one inch in width, depending upon the texture of the material. Fabrics finished with dressing, such as percale or cambric, will work successfully when cut $\frac{7}{8}''$ wide, while soft material such as batiste, lawn or

FIG. 24a. ATTACHING BIAS GAUGE TO SCISSORS   FIG. 24b. CUTTING BIAS STRIPS

silk must measure from $\frac{15}{16}''$ to one inch in width. A trial with the Binder will quickly determine the proper width for the material to be used. When binding is cut too narrow the edges will not turn in, and if too wide, will fold over in plaits.

The cutting gauge will insure an even width of binding and a quantity can be cut in a short time.

Joining Bias Strips

One yard of yard-wide material will make about 30 yards of bias strips $\frac{7}{8}''$ wide. It is usually an economy to purchase this amount and save any surplus for future use.

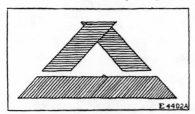
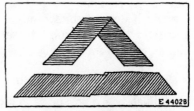

FIG. 25a. THE RIGHT WAY TO   FIG. 25b. THE WRONG WAY TO
        JOIN STRIPS   JOIN STRIPS

Cut the strips, lay the two diagonal ends together, as shown in Fig. 25a, and stitch the ends together. The stitching should be as close to the edge as possible so that the seam will pass through the Binder freely. When the strips are straightened out, as shown in Fig. 25a, the edges will be exactly even. Do not join the strips as shown in Fig. 25b, as the edges will be uneven when straightened

20

out. It is advisable to press the seams open with an iron and if the strips are not to be used immediately they should be wound on a piece of cardboard to keep them from stretching.

Attaching the Binder to the Machine

Raise the needle to the highest point and remove the presser foot from the machine by loosening the thumb screw which holds it in place. Compare the foot of the Binder and the presser foot and you will see that they are attached to the machine in the same manner. Attach the Binder to the presser bar. Turn the balance wheel slowly toward you to make sure that the Binder is properly attached to the bar and that the needle goes through the center of the needle hole.

THE BINDER

Inserting the Binding in the Binder

Cut the binding to a long point to left, as shown. Insert the pointed end in the binder scroll, Fig. 27, until the pointed end comes through the lower end of the scroll.

CUTTING POINT
ON BINDING

FIG. 27. INSERTING BINDING IN BINDER

Pull the binding through under the presser foot before starting to sew. Note that as the binding passes through the scroll of the Binder the edges are turned in.

21

Binding May be Purchased Cut and Folded
for Use with the Binder

Folded bias binding may be purchased for use with the Binder. This binding comes in a variety of materials and colors. Folded bindings for use with the Binder must measure ½" in width. The No. 5 width in standard brands usually measures ½",

FIG. 28. INSERT FOLDED BINDING IN OUTSIDE SLOT

but it is always well to be sure of this before purchasing.

Folded binding is inserted in the outside slot of the Binder, as shown in Fig. 28. The Binder is adjusted and operated in the same manner as when using unfolded binding. One-half inch braid or ribbon may be used in the same manner.

A binding inserted in the outside slot of the Binder will be turned only once. It is therefore necessary to have finished edges when using binding in this slot.

The Adjustment and Operation of the Binder

The edge to be bound should be held well within the center slot of the scroll, (A, Fig. 29). If the material is allowed to slip away from the scroll when near the needle, the edge will not be caught in the binding. With a little practice it is quite easy to hold the edge in the scroll.

Various materials and conditions require different adjustments of the Binder to bring the stitching close to the edge. A wider adjustment of the Binder is required when binding curves than is necessary when binding a straight edge.

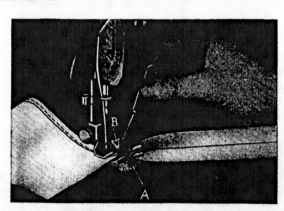

FIG. 29. ADJUSTING THE BINDER

To adjust the Binder for stitching, loosen screw B, Fig. 29, and move scroll to the right for a narrower adjustment and to the left for a wider adjustment. Care should be taken to see that the screw is well tightened after making an adjustment. To become perfectly familiar with the adjustment of the Binder, practice is necessary.

Binding Outside Curves

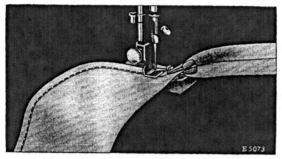

FIG. 30. BINDING AN OUTSIDE CURVE

Practice is required to bind a curved edge properly. The edge to be bound must be allowed to pass freely through the scroll and should not be crowded against the wall of it. Guiding should be from the back of the binder and to the left, allowing unfinished edges to swing naturally into the scroll of the binder.

Never pull the binding as it feeds through the Binder, as bias material is very easily stretched and will be too narrow when it reaches the needle. When this occurs the edges will not be turned.

When binding a curved edge (see Fig. 30), turn the material only as fast as the machine sews. It is not possible to hold the material in the entire length of the scroll when binding a small curve.

Do not push the material in too fast, as the edge will then become puckered, and do not stretch the material or the curve will not be the proper shape when finished. If the stitching does not catch the edge of the binding the scroll should be adjusted a trifle to the left.

FIG. 31. SAMPLE OF OUT SIDE CURVE

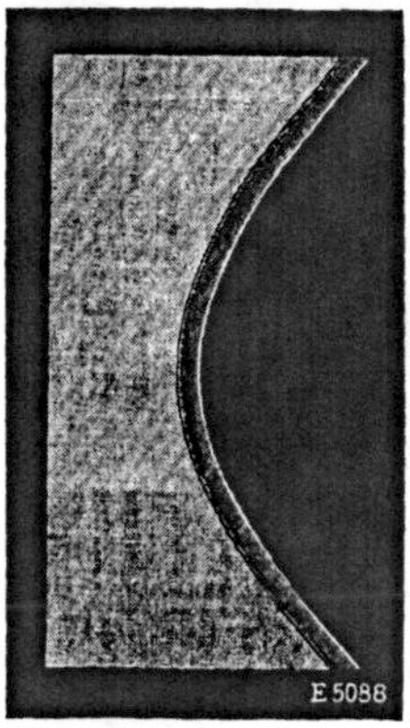

Binding Inside Curves

It will be necessary to practice binding an inside curve on various kinds of material, as this curve is found on nearly all garments which may be finished with a bound edge.

When binding an inside curve with the Binder, straighten out the edge as it is being fed into the attachment. When doing this, care should be taken not to stretch the edge of the material.

If the material is soft, like batiste or crepe de chine, add a row of machine stitching close to the edge of the curve before binding.

FIG. 32. SAMPLE OF INSIDE CURVE

23

Applying a French Fold to a Curve

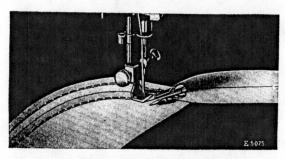

FIG. 33. APPLYING FRENCH FOLDS

A French fold is applied by placing the material under the attachment and stitching the binding in position as shown in Fig. 33. A line made by basting or with chalk or pencil may be used as a guide in applying rows where wanted.

Binding a Square Corner

To bind a square corner, apply the binding along one side to within ⅛″ of edge of the material, stopping the machine with the needle and take-up at the highest point. Then draw the material back away from the needle far enough to pull about two inches of the binding through the Binder. Fold and crease the binding to a square mitered corner, turn the material and draw it back into the Binder, bringing the needle down through the binding close to the corner, as shown in Fig. 34. Draw the slack thread back through the needle and tension. Be sure the new edge of

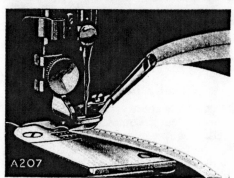

FIG. 34. TURNING A SQUARE CORNER

FIG. 35. SAMPLE OF SQUARE CORNER

the material is properly placed in the scroll of the Binder and begin stitching slowly until you are sure the material is feeding properly. The loop of the thread on the underside at the corner may be tied or cut off without fear of ravelling, as the stitched is locked.

Binding Plackets

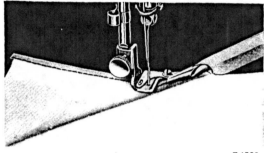

FIG. 36. BINDING A PLACKET

To bind a placket, stitch down the left side of slit until the point of placket is about to enter scroll. Then swing right side of slit sharply into a straight line, the fullness of the material forming a V at left.

Run the machine slowly as the point is reached and take care that too much material is not allowed to feed into the Binder.

For practice, cut a slit about five inches deep in muslin and learn to fold it in a straight line before starting to bind. When you have mastered the placket you will find it quite easy to bind scallops.

Bound Scallops

The same method used in binding an outside curve is used for binding scallops and the point at the top of the scallop is bound in exactly the same manner as the placket. Practice the binding of a small single scallop first before attempting to bind a row of scallops.

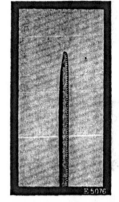

FIG. 37. SAMPLE OF BOUND PLACKET

If the material is soft and liable to stretch add a row of machine stitching close to the edge of the scallop before starting to bind the edge.

Applying Military Braid with the Binder

Military braid ½″ in width may be used in the Binder by inserting it in the outside slot of the scroll, following directions for using **folded** binding on page 22.

This braid makes a suitable trimming for serge or other woolen material and, when applied with the Binder, has a neat tailored

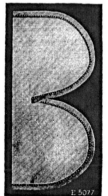

FIG. 38. SAMPLE OF BOUND SCALLOPS

appearince impossible to obtain by hand sewing.

Both inside and outside curves may be bound with perfect ease after the Binder has been properly adjusted.

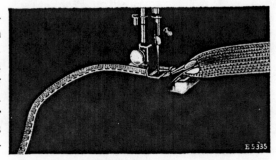

Fig. 39. Binding with Military Braid

Binding and Applying Rick-Rack Braid to the Edge of a Garment at One Stitching

Rick-Rack braid may be purchased at any notion counter and comes in a variety of colors and widths. This braid makes an attractive trimming for house dresses and aprons and may be applied to an outside or an inside curve at the same time the edge is bound.

Insert the edge to be bound, together with the rick-rack braid in the scroll of the Binder, as shown in Fig. 40.

Fig. 40. Binding and Applying Rick-Rack Braid

The rick-rack braid should be fed into the binder in a straight line and against the wall of the scroll, regardless of the shape of the garment to which it is being attached. This is especially true when binding an outside curve.

An attractive finish may be given by applying a second row of rick-rack to the free edge of the binding, using the presser foot.

26

Making Button Loops with the Binder

To make button loops, first stitch together a piece of binding of the desired material and length by using the Binder. You will then have a quarter-inch fold with the edges stitched together.

Cut a strip of binding long enough to make a loop of the desired size and fold it to a point by bringing the two stitched edges together having ends even, being careful to keep right side upper-

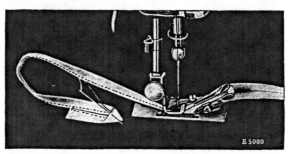

FIG. 41. MAKING BUTTON LOOPS

most. Fasten the loop at the point with a hand sewing needle.

These loops are most attractive when made of silk material or military braid and may be applied in various ways to the frock or blouse.

Bound Buttonholes Made with the Binder

Take a strip of material as wide as you wish to make your buttonholes apart and bind each side. For example, if you wish to make your buttonholes two inches apart take a two-inch strip of material as shown in Fig. 42, at A, and bind each side as shown at B.

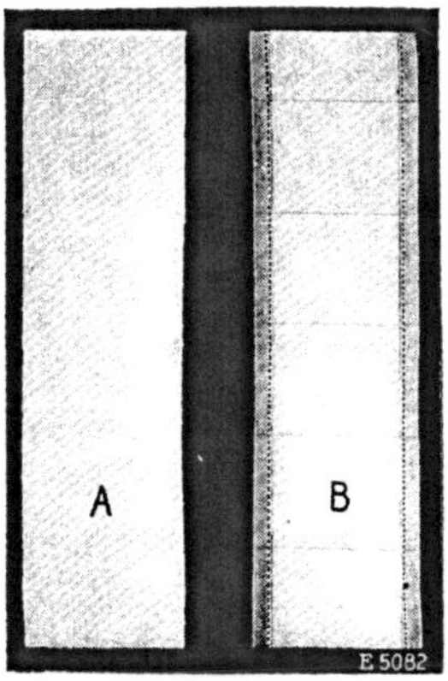

Measure the diameter of the button you wish to use and cut the bound strip into pieces one-half inch wider than the button. See Fig. 42-B. After the strip is cut into sections, bind them together so that the bound edges just meet, as shown in Fig. 43. Bind one edge of this strip, using the Binder, and before binding the other edge, place the edge of the garment even with the strip of buttonholes and bind both edges at one stitching. See Fig. 44. The free edge of the binding can then be stitched flat to the garment.

FIG. 42. STARTING BOUND
BUTTONHOLES

27

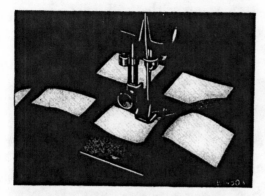

FIG. 43. BINDING PIECES TOGETHER

If an extra-strong buttonhole is desired, a linen tape may be used for the binding. This must, however, be one-half inch in width and be used in the outside slot of the Binder.

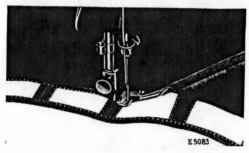

FIG. 44. COMPLETING BOUND BUTTONHOLES

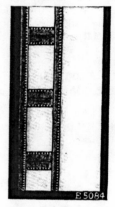

FIG. 45. SAMPLE OF BOUND BUTTONHOLES

Suggested List of Garments that May be Finished with Binding

The edge of cooking aprons and caps.

Percale kitchen aprons.

Dust caps.

Iron holders.

The neck and sleeves of night gowns—narrow lace may be applied to edge of binding by hand or machine.

The edge of chemise—binding may be decorated with feather stitching or French knots.

The edges of underwaists for children—the buttonholes may also be made with the Binder.

Plackets on underwear.

Rompers for children—edges of garment and buttonholes.

Children's dresses of gingham or print.

Boys' sailor suits—collar and cuffs bound and trimmed with French folds.

Organdie dresses—edges bound and French folds applied.

Button loops for cotton or silk dresses.

Cut-in buttonholes for tailored garments.

Rick-rack braid and binding for house dresses and aprons.

Military braid for finishing the edge of serge or other woolen dresses or coats.

Bound scallops for underwear or dresses.

Bound scallops for bed spreads or curtains.

Bound tabs for tailored dresses.

NEW USES FOR THE FOOT HEMMER AND THE ADJUSTABLE HEMMER

The Foot Hemmer

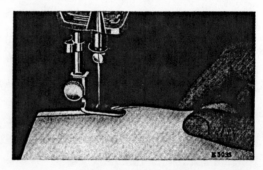

FIG. 46. THE FOOT HEMMER

The Foot Hemmer (Fig. 46) is attached to the machine in place of the presser foot. Raise the needle to the highest point, loosen the thumb screw which clamps the presser foot to the presser bar and remove the presser foot. Attach the Foot Hemmer to the bar, taking care to tighten the screw firmly so that the Hemmer will not become loose when the machine is running. Turn the balance wheel slowly to make sure that the needle goes through the center of the needle hole and that the lower thread is properly pulled up.

How to Start the Hem at the Very Edge

How to start the hem at the very edge of the material is of great importance in learning to use the Hemmer. If the hem is not started at the edge and the material is pulled bias a perfect hem cannot be made.

There are several ways of starting the hem at the edge, but the most practical one is as follows:

1. Fold over about ⅛″ of the edge of the material at the starting point for a distance of about one inch.

2. Place the material in the Hemmer at an angle leading to the right at a point just beyond the fold.

3. Draw the material toward you through the Hemmer, as shown in Fig. 47, at the same time

FIG. 47. STARTING A HEM AT THE EDGE

making the second fold at the very edge. Continue to draw the material through the Hemmer until the edge is just under the needle. Place the upper and lower threads together under the Hemmer foot and assist in starting of the hem by slightly pulling the threads from the back as the machine is run.

Making a Hem with the Foot Hemmer

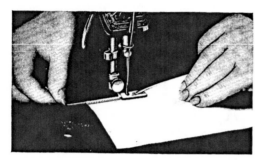

FIG. 48.   MAKING A HEM WITH THE FOOT HEMMER

The same width of material must be kept in the Hemmer at all times. After placing the correct width of material in the Hemmer hold it in a straight line and you will find it quite easy to make a perfect hem. See Fig. 48.

Making a Hemmed Seam with the Foot Hemmer

The hemmed seam is very practical to use on underwear, or in fact on any garment where a straight seam is used and where a small double seam would be suitable.

When using this seam the garment must first be fitted and the edge of the material trimmed, allowing for about one-eighth inch seam. The two edges are placed together and inserted in the Hemmer in the same manner as a single hem. If the material is bulky, the edge of the upper piece of material may be placed about one-eighth inch in from the edge of the lower piece. See Fig. 49.

The free edge of a hemmed seam may be stitched flat to the garment if desired. First open the work out flat, then place the hem in the scroll of the Hemmer, which acts as a guide, holding the edge of the hem in position while it is being stitched.

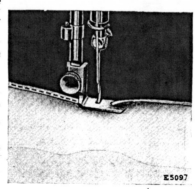

FIG. 49.   MAKING A HEMMED SEAM

If the seam is stitched flat to the garment one row of stitching is visible on the right side.

The hemmed seam may be used on muslin, lawn, percale, organdie or other fine materials where a narrow seam is desirable.

Hemming and Sewing on Lace at One Operation

Start the hem in the regular way and with the needle holding the hem in position, raise the presser bar sufficiently to allow the edge of the lace to be slipped in under the Foot Hemmer, at the same time bringing it up through the slot at the right of the Hemmer. See Fig. 50. Lower the bar, turn the balance wheel and catch the edge of the lace with the needle. Guide the hem with the right hand and the lace with the left. Care should be taken not to stretch the lace as it is being fed into the Hemmer.

It is not practical to sew gathered lace on with the Foot Hemmer, as the fulled lace catches in the Hemmer slot.

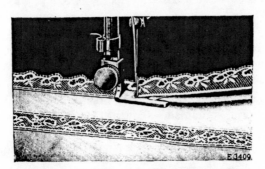

FIG. 50. HEMMING AND SEWING ON LACE

A very attractive way of applying lace so that the stitching of the hem is not visible is to start the hem in the regular way, slipping the lace in from the left as you would the second piece of material when making a hemmed seam.

Hemming Fine Materials with the Foot Hemmer

When hemming fine materials such as georgette or crepe de chine with the Foot Hemmer, the material will not feed through properly and the stitch will be very much shorter than when sewing with the presser foot on the same material.

To overcome this difficulty, and to assist in holding soft materials so that they will be turned properly with the Foot Hemmer, insert a piece of paper under the foot of the Hemmer and allow it to feed through with the material. Strips of thin paper or the edges of newspaper are very convenient for stitching. Never use tissue paper, as this will be very difficult to pull away from the material.

32

The Adjustable Hemmer

The Adjustable Hemmer (Fig. 51) is a part of the set of attachments supplied with most family machines. This Hemmer will make a hem of any desired width up to one inch. For wider hems, the scale may be released and thrown out of position.

Fig. 51. The Adjust-
able Hemmer

Remove the presser foot and attach the Hemmer to the presser bar, taking care that the needle comes in the center of the needle hole after you tighten the thumb screw.

How to Adjust the Hemmer for Hems of Various Widths

To adjust the Hemmer loosen the screw and you will then be able to move the hemmer guide to the right or to the left. Note the pointer (A, Fig. 51) which is used in connection with the scale of figures on the Adjustable Hemmer.

The Hemmer may be adjusted as follows:

Pointer set at:

1—for $\frac{1}{8}''$ hem (approximate)   5—for $\frac{5}{8}''$ hem (approximate)
2— " $\frac{1}{4}''$ " "   6— " $\frac{3}{4}''$ " "
3— " $\frac{3}{8}''$ " "   7— " $\frac{7}{8}''$ " "
4— " $\frac{1}{2}''$ " "   8— " $1''$ " "

After setting the Hemmer, care should be taken to see that the adjusting screw is well tightened before starting to sew.

How to Insert the Material in the Adjustable Hemmer

Fold over the edge at the end of the material to be hemmed, as instructed for starting a hem with the Foot Hemmer. Place the material in the Hemmer under the scale and draw it back and forth until the hem is formed.

You will then be able to determine the width and to fold over the end of the hem for the second turning. Draw the material back until the end comes directly under the needle.

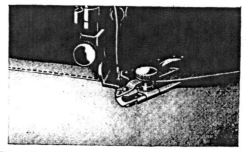

Fig. 52. Hemming with Adjustable Hemmer

Lower the presser bar and sew, guiding sufficient material in the Hemmer to turn the hem properly. See Fig. 52.

If the hem is not started at the edge it will run bias and not come out even at the other end.

Hemming Soft Material

When hemming soft material that is liable to stretch it is well to slip a piece of paper under the Hemmer next to the feed. This will prevent the material from stretching and assist in turning the hem.

How to Prepare a Hem on Table Linen

Much time is spent in turning the hem of table linen to make it ready for hand sewing. The Hemmer is very valuable for this operation. Set the Hemmer for the desired width hem, take the thread from the needle and run the linen through the Hemmer.

You will find that the hem has been evenly turned, ready for the hand sewing and the holes made by the machine needle have softened the linen, making it quite easy to do the hand work. See Fig. 53.

Table linen or other material may be prepared for hemstitching in this manner.

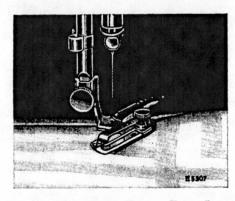

Fig. 53. Preparing a Hem on Table Linen

Making a Wide Hem with the Adjustable Hemmer

To make a hem wider than one inch with the Adjustable Hemmer, loosen adjusting screw and throw scale guide out of position. Attach the foot section to the machine, crease the hem for the desired width and insert the edge in the Hemmer. The Hemmer will turn the edge and stitch it flat, but the operator must keep the crease for the width of the hem even as the machine sews. Hems may be applied to sheets or other similar articles in this manner.

34

The French Way of Applying Lace

A very attractive way of applying lace so that the stitching of the hem is not visible is to start the hem in the regular way, slipping the lace in from the left as you would the second piece of material when making a hemmed seam. See Fig. 88.

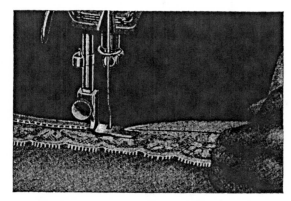

FIG. 88. APPLYING LACE THE FRENCH WAY

Suggested List of Garments on which the Hemmers may be Used

Kitchen and hand towels.

Muslin curtains.

The edges of ruffles or flounces for lingerie dresses or underwear.

Hemming and sewing on lace for ruffles.

Setting in lace insertion for underwear or children's clothes.

Percale or gingham kitchen aprons.

Bottom edge of men's shirts.

Edges of silk underwear.

Apron strings of lawn, percale or gingham.

Baby bonnet strings.

Ruffles for boudoir pillows.

Seams on heavy material to prevent fraying.

Sheets—small and wide hem.

Table linen—hem turned, ready for hand sewing.

Over drapes of cretonne.

Plaitings of lawn or organdie for dresses or collar sets.

DAINTY WAYS TO USE THE TUCKER

Tucking is the natural trimming for fine materials such as lawn, organdie, batiste, etc., and may be made without basting in any width from a fine pin tuck to one inch wide when using the Singer Tucker. The Tucker gauges the width of the tuck and while one tuck is being stitched the mark for the next tuck is being made.

It is so simple to make tucks in this way that it is a joy to plan garments with this fascinating trimming. Then, too, such trimmings may be made without extra cost. The fashion magazines always give numerous suggestions for tucking various garments. The following pages will explain the adjusting and operating of this time-saving attachment.

The Parts of the Tucker and Their Uses

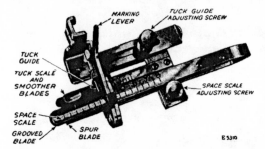

Select the Tucker from the box of attachments, compare it with Fig. 54 and note the names and uses of the various parts, as follows:

Fig. 54. THE TUCKER AND ITS WORKING PARTS

The Tuck Guide, which is adjustable and may be set for any desired width of tuck.

The Tuck Scale, containing figures which indicate different widths of tucks. The tuck scale also acts as a smoother blade, keeping the tucks of uniform width.

The Tuck Guide Adjusting Screw, by means of which the tuck guide may be set at any point on the tuck scale.

The Space Scale, containing figures on the upper blade which indicate the width of the space between tucks. The middle or **grooved blade** contains a groove into which the material is pressed by the **spur** at the end of the lower or **spur blade,** thus marking the goods for the folding of the next tuck.

The Space Scale Adjusting Screw, by means of which the space scale may be set at any desired point.

The Marking Lever, which presses on the grooved blade, marking the material as it passes between the grooved and spur blades.

A careful study of the Tucker parts and their relations to each other before using this attachment will make its operation quite clear.

Where to Oil the Tucker

The only place on the Tucker that requires oiling is the stud on which the marking lever works. See Fig. 56. One drop of oil occasionally is sufficient. Careless oiling will result in oily blades and soiled material. When the marking lever does not move up and down freely it requires oiling. If neglected it may become so dry that it will stay down and cause a drag on the material instead of lifting freely as the mark is made.

To Attach the Tucker to the Machine

Raise the needle bar to the highest point, remove the presser foot from the machine and attach the Tucker in its place. Care should be taken to see that the Tucker is securely fastened to the presser bar and that the needle goes through the center of the needle hole. Note the position of the marking lever, making sure that it is in the lower position and that the needle clamp works on it as the machine sews.

How to Adjust the Scales on the Tucker

The width of the tucks and the space between them is determined by the adjustment of the scales. Adjustment for width of tuck is made by loosening the tuck guide adjusting screw, which allows you to move the tuck guide to the desired figure on the tuck scale. The tuck guide should be set just over the figure you wish to use. The adjusting screw should always be well tightened.

FIG. 55. TUCKER SET AT PIN TUCK AND 2 SPACE

To adjust for the width of space between the tucks, loosen the space scale adjusting screw and move the space scale until the desired figure is directly in a line with the center of the needle hole. You will find a line in front and back of the needle hole to indicate the center.

Before starting to sew, tighten the screw well to prevent the scale shifting when the Tucker is in operation.

The figures on the tuck scale indicate the width of tuck in eighths of an inch, the marks between figures are sixteenths.

The marks on the space scale are double the width of those on the tuck scale, so that when both scales are set at the same figure, blind tucks without spaces between them are made.

To make space between tucks, first set the tuck scale, then move the space scale to the same number and as much farther to the left as you wish to have space. Each number on the space scale represents one-quarter of an inch and each mark between numbers one-eighth of an inch.

Use the table below to assist you in setting the Tucker.

	TUCK GUIDE	SPACE SCALE
$\frac{1}{8}''$ tucks with no space	1	1
$\frac{1}{8}''$ " " $\frac{1}{8}''$ "	1	$1\frac{1}{2}$
$\frac{1}{4}''$ " " no "	2	2
$\frac{1}{4}''$ " " $\frac{1}{4}''$ "	2	3
$\frac{1}{2}''$ " " no "	4	4
$\frac{1}{2}''$ " " $\frac{1}{2}''$ "	4	6
$1''$ " " no "	8	8

Note Fig. 55, showing Tucker set at a pin tuck and 2 for space.

Where to Insert the Material to be Tucked

Fold and crease the first tuck for its entire length by hand, insert it in the Tucker from the left, placing it between the grooved blade and the spur blade of the space scale, and between the two blades of the tuck scale. See Fig. 56.

FIG. 56. PROPER POSITION OF MATERIAL IN TUCKER

Care should be taken to see that the material is placed far enough in the Tucker to feed against the tuck guide. Draw the material towards you until the edge is directly under the needle. Lower the presser bar and sew. You will note that the Tucker is now making a mark for the next tuck.

When the first tuck is finished, fold the material on the mark made by the spur during the sewing of the first tuck and insert the folded edge in the Tucker. It is most important to see that the first tuck is against the inside of the spur. After lowering the presser bar, raise the material slightly and adjust it until the folded edge is just touching the guide and the preceding tuck is against the spur. This insures even tucks.

How to Tuck Silk or Chiffon

It is possible to tuck silks, such as taffeta, quite as easily as cotton material. Soft materials such as crepe de chine and georgette are harder to crease, but may be tucked successfully if a piece of paper is slipped under the Tucker. It is quite necessary that the tensions be properly adjusted before starting to tuck fine materials, as a tight tension will pucker the material and cause the thread to break when the tuck is pressed.

How to Make Fine Tucks and Cross Tucking

When making fine tucks it is quite necessary to use thread of the proper size to suit the material to be tucked. A fine needle, fine thread and a fine stitch are the secrets of attractive tucking. Many ready-made garments trimmed with tucking are unattractive because the thread and stitches are too coarse.

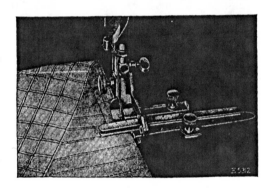

Always test your tensions on a piece of the same material you wish to tuck and be sure they are properly adjusted before tucking a garment.

FIG. 57. CROSS TUCKING

When making cross tucking, first decide on the combination of tuck and space you wish to use, and set the Tucker. Tuck the entire piece of material lengthwise, then crosswise over the tucks. See Fig. 57. Care should be taken to see that the tucks lie in the proper direction before starting to cross the tucks. It is well to press the tucks with an iron before the cross tucks are made to prevent the material from becoming bias as it is tucked.

Attractive cross tucking may also be made by first tucking the material lengthwise and then bias across the tucks.

39

 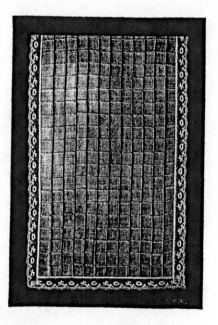

SAMPLE OF FINE TUCKING   SAMPLE OF CROSS TUCKING

Suggested List of Practical Uses of the Tucker

Tucking underwear of silk or cotton.
Lingerie frocks.
Children's dresses.
Baby bonnets.
Collar and cuff sets.
Tea aprons.
Shirt waist fronts.
Cross-tucked bands for lingerie and underwear.
Tucked medallions for underwear.
Pin tucks on ruffles for underwear.
Cross-tucked pillow tops.
Wide tucks for frocks.
Tucked bands for blouses and underwear.
Taffeta and crepe de chine dresses.

THE MANY PRACTICAL USES OF THE RUFFLER

Ruffling has played an important part in trimming garments for centuries past, but the modern way to make and apply these trimmings is quite different from the method our grandmothers used. The Ruffler furnished with Singer Family Sewing Machines will make ruffles of any desired fullness at a speed of ten yards in ten minutes, and by a simple adjustment the ruffles may be changed to dainty plaitings. This attachment is a wonderful time saver when making trimmings and is so simple to use that by carefully following the directions given in this book perfect results may be obtained.

The Parts of the Ruffler and Their Uses

It is necessary to become familiar with the Ruffler before it can be used successfully. Select the Ruffler from the set of attachments and compare it with Fig. 58. Note the names and uses of the principal parts, as follows:

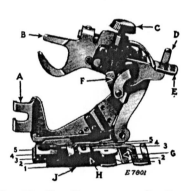

FIG. 58. THE RUFFLER AND ITS PARTS

NOTE: If the Ruffler with your machine is not exactly like Fig. 58, you will find the working parts quite similar. Any difference in the adjustments will be found explained in the instruction book. The 66-1 Singer machine has an entirely different type of foot from other Singer models and it is well to compare the foot on the Ruffler with the presser foot before attempting to attach the Ruffler to the machine.

A—**Foot**—the part by which the ruffler is attached to the presser bar.

B—**Fork Arm**—the section that must be placed astride the needle clamp.

C—**Adjusting Screw**—the screw that regulates the fullness of the gather.

D—**Projection**—the part that projects through the slots in the adjusting lever.

E—**Adjusting Lever**—the lever that sets the ruffler for gathering or for making a plait once at every six stitches or once at every twelve stitches, as desired; also for disengaging the ruffler, when either plaiting or gathering is not desired.

41

F—Adjusting Finger—the part which regulates the width or size of the plaits.

G—Separator Guide—the guide on the underside of the ruffler, containing slots into which the edge of the material is placed to keep the heading of the ruffle even; also for separating the material to be ruffled from the material to which the ruffle is to be attached.

H—Ruffling Blade—the upper blue steel blade with the teeth at the end to push the material in plaits up to the needle.

J—Separator Blade—the lower blue steel blade without teeth, which prevents the teeth of the ruffling blade coming into contact with the feed of the machine, or the material to which ruffle or plaiting is to be applied.

Lines 1, 2, 3, 4 and 5 (Fig. 58) indicate where the material is to be placed for various operations, as follows:

Line 1—the proper position for the material to which the ruffle is applied.

Line 2—the material to be gathered.

Line 3—the facing for the ruffle.

Line 4—the strip of piping material.

Line 5—the edge to be piped.

Refer to this illustration when inserting the material in the Ruffler.

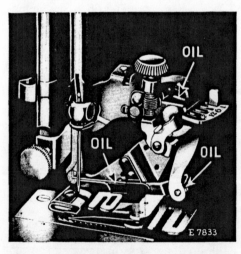

FIG. 59. OILING POINTS ON RUFFLER

Oiling the Ruffler

The Ruffler requires an occasional oiling of all working parts to prevent them from sticking. A drop of oil at each point indicated in Fig. 59 is sufficient. If possible, sew on a waste piece of material after oiling to prevent your garment from becoming soiled. If the Ruffler does not plait evenly a drop of oil may remedy the trouble.

Attaching the Ruffler to the Machine

Raise the needle bar to the highest point and remove the presser foot. Attach the ruffler foot to the bar, at the same time placing the fork-arm astride the needle clamp. Turn the balance wheel slowly by hand to see that the needle comes down in the center of the needle hole.

Adjusting the Ruffler for Plain Gather

The adjusting finger (F, Fig. 60) is not intended for gathering and should be moved forward or away from the needle, as shown in Fig. 60.

Raise the adjusting lever (E, Fig. 60) and move it to the left so that the projection (D, Fig. 60) will enter the slot marked "1" in the adjusting lever (E) when the lever is released. The Ruffling Blade will then move forward and back once at every stitch. Insert the material to be ruffled between the two blue blades, following the line 2 in Fig. 58. Draw the material slightly back of the needle, lower the presser bar and commence to sew.

To make fine gathering, shorten the stroke of the ruffling blade by turning the adjusting screw (C, Fig. 60) upwardly, also shorten the stitch. To make full gathering, lengthen the stroke of the ruffling blade by turning the adjusting screw (C) downwardly, also lengthen the stitch. By varying these adjustments, many pleasing varieties of work can be accomplished.

Inserting the Material in the Ruffler and Making a Plain Gather

For ruffling or gathering, the adjusting finger should be released or turned toward the operator.

Insert the material in the Ruffler between the two blue blades following line 2, Fig. 58. Pull the edge of the material to be gathered forward until it is slightly past the needle, lower the presser bar and sew. See Fig. 60. The fullness of the ruffle is determined by the position of the adjust-

FIG. 60. MAKING A PLAIN GATHER

ing screw. To **decrease** the fullness turn the screw **up.** To **increase** the fullness turn the screw **down.**

43

Making a Ruffle and Sewing It to the Garment at One Operation

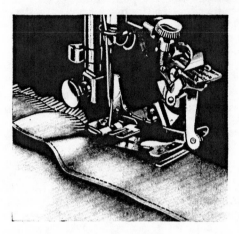

After having tested and adjusted the Ruffler for fullness, place the material for the ruffle in the Ruffler between the two blue blades and insert the garment to which it is to be attached under the separator blade following line 1, Fig. 58. Proceed as for plain gathering, guiding the material lightly so that it will not feed away from the heading guide. See Fig. 61.

FIG. 61. MAKING A RUFFLE AND SEWING IT TO THE GARMENT

A Facing May be Added at the Same Time the Ruffle is Made

First insert the material for the ruffle in the Ruffler between the two blades and the garment under the separator blade, as directed for sewing the ruffle to the garment in one operation. Place the material for the facing in the Ruffler, following line 3, Fig. 58. The facing may be straight or bias material. If the facing is to be on the right side of the garment, place the garment and the ruffle so that the wrong sides are together. If the facing is to be on the wrong side, place the right sides of the garment and the ruffle together. See Fig. 62.

FIG. 62. ADDING A FACING AS THE RUFFLE IS MADE

Applying Rows of Ruffles to a Garment

Rows of ruffles may be stitched to a garment at the same time the material is ruffled by placing the garment under the Ruffler and the material for the ruffle between the blades, as shown in Fig. 63. The position on the garment for the ruffles may be indicated by a basting thread or a chalk mark.

FIG. 63. APPLYING ROWS OF RUFFLES TO A GARMENT

If the heading on the ruffle is to be more than one-quarter of an inch wide, do not place the material in the guide when following line 2 (Fig. 58) but place the edge of the ruffle between the blades and to the right of the needle the desired amount, up to one inch, and guide it as the machine sews.

The edges of the ruffles may be hemmed with the foot hemmer or picoted on a special power hemstitching machine. The addition of a narrow lace edge is often attractive.

Adjusting the Ruffler for Plaiting

For plaiting, the adjusting finger should be set into position under adjusting screw; the projection in the slot marked 6 or the slot marked 12 in the adjusting lever. The adjusting screw on the Ruffler must be turned down as far as it will go when plaiting. To make the plaits farther apart, **lengthen** the stitch on the sewing machine. To make them closer together, **shorten** the stitch. Any material with dressing,

FIG. 64. THE RUFFLER ADJUSTED FOR PLAITING

such as lawn, organdie or taffeta, may be successfully plaited with the Ruffler. Softer materials may be plaited but the plaits will not lie flat unless they are very well pressed.

Plaiting may be applied to the garment at the same time it is made, following directions on page 44. A facing may also be applied as illustrated on page 44.

To Adjust the Ruffler for
Group Plaiting and Gathering

The ruffler can be adjusted for group plaiting by lifting the adjusting lever (E, Fig. 65) and moving it to the right so that the top of the projection (D, Fig. 65) rests on the small slot indicated by the star on the adjusting lever. This should be done at the points where you wish to make the space between the plaits. The ruffler will then stop and plain stitching will be made. When the desired space has been made, adjust the lever (E) so that the projection (D) enters either the slot marked "6" or the slot marked "12."

FIG. 65.   GROUP PLAITING

By alternately making groups of plaits and plain spaces, as shown in Fig. 65, very attractive work can be produced.

How to Test the Ruffle for Fullness

It is often necessary to adjust the Ruffler for a certain fullness, but because the length of stitch affects the fullness as well as the position of the adjusting screw, it is impossible to have an indicator on the Ruffler to determine the amount of fullness that will be taken up. In addition, some materials take up more fullness than others with the same setting of the stitch and adjusting screw. It is therefore necessary to experiment with a small piece of the material to be ruffled if the correct amount is to be gathered. For example, if the fullness of a ruffle is to be one and a-half, take a six-inch piece of material and gather it into a four-inch space.

How to Slide the Gathers on the Thread

Another convenient way to gather to fit a given space is to loosen the upper tension on the machine. This will allow the gathers to slide on the thread to fit the desired space the same as in hand gathering.

When gathering it this way it is necessary to leave a long thread when taking the material from the machine so that the gathers may be adjusted as desired. It is also well to use a strong upper thread so that there will be no danger of breaking it when sliding the gathers.

Finishing a Ruffled Seam with Binding

Make the ruffle and sew it to the garment in one operation, then trim the seam close to the edge. Remove the Ruffler and attach the Binder to the machine. Select a suitable material to use for binding the seam and insert it in the Binder. Place the edge of the ruffled seam in the Binder and bind as shown in Fig. 66.

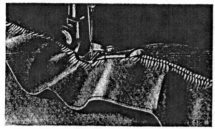

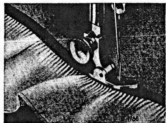

FIG. 66. FINISHING A RUFFLED SEAM WITH BINDING

FIG. 67. BINDING A RUFFLED SEAM FLAT

The seam may be bound on the right side of the garment if desired and then stitched flat as shown in Fig. 67.

Finishing a Ruffle with a French Seam

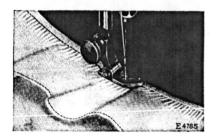

FIG. 68. RUFFLE FINISHED WITH A FRENCH SEAM

Place the garment and the material for the ruffle in the Ruffler as previously explained, with the wrong side of the material to be ruffled facing the wrong side of the garment. After sewing the ruffle to the garment in one operation, trim the seam close to the line of stitching and turn the seam to the wrong side of the garment. Stitch in position with the presser foot. See Fig. 68.

Plaited Lace or Ribbon

Ribbon and lace that has a little dressing can be plaited successfully with the Ruffler, if one inch or more in width. When plaiting lace, however, it is necessary to place a strip of paper under the Ruffler. See Fig. 69 and note especially the paper under the Ruffler. Ribbon is plaited in the same manner, but paper is not required unless the ribbon is very soft.

It is advisable to use lace with a fine mesh for plaiting because coarse lace may catch in the ruffling blade.

Very attractive trimmings for lingerie and fancy articles may be made of plaited lace. Rosettes of lace or ribbon are used for decoration on many garments.

FIG. 69. PLAITING LACE WITH PAPER

47

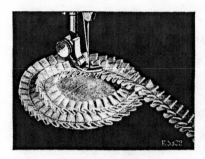

FIG. 70. MAKING ROSETTES

Rosettes of Plaiting

Rosettes of plaited ribbon or silk for trimming dresses or fancy articles for use in the home are very easily and quickly made with the Ruffler. Ribbon of ¾″ or more in width, and with sufficient body to hold a plait, may be plaited with the Ruffler. The plaiting is then sewn to a circle of crinoline, using the presser foot. See Fig. 70.

Puffed Ribbon

Puffed ribbon makes a most attractive trimming and may be of one-inch ribbon or wider. Adjust the Ruffler for the desired fullness and insert the edge of the ribbon in the Ruffler as for plain gathering. After gathering one edge, place the other edge in the Ruffler and gather in the same manner. A loose upper tension may be

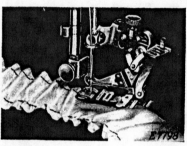

FIG. 71. MAKING PUFFED RIBBON

used to allow the pulling up of the ribbon to the desired length. See Fig. 71.

Puffed ribbon makes very attractive trimming for couch pillows.

Suggested List of Garments that May be Trimmed with Ruffling or Plaiting

Lingerie.
Petticoats and bloomers for children.
Frocks of cotton or silk.
Puffing for taffeta dresses.
House dresses.
Shirt waists.
Tea aprons.
Collar and cuff sets.
Plaiting or puffing for overskirts and flounces.
Plaiting or puffing for ends of sash.
Plaited ribbon for hats.
Puffing for baby bonnets.
Ruffles for boudoir pillows.
Puffing for sofa pillows.
Fancy lamp shades.
Puffing or plaiting for children's hats.

Relative Sizes of Needles and Thread

(Class and Variety of Needles Used, 15 x 1)

Sizes of Needles	Classes of Work	Sizes of Cotton, Silk or Linen Thread
9	Georgette, chiffon, light-weight rayon, fine dimity, lawn, batiste and other feather-weight or sheer fabrics. For infants' clothes and for dainty lingerie, also fine lace and all delicate or gossamer fabrics.	100 to 150 Cotton OO & OOO Silk Twist
11	All medium light-weight, summertime fabrics. For children's clothes, dainty house dresses and aprons, glass curtains.	80 to 100 Cotton O Silk Twist
14	Light-weight woolens, firm dress silks and cottons, draperies and fabric furnishings. For smocks and men's fine shirts. For general household sewing; for fine quilting.	60 to 80 Cotton A & B Silk Twist
16	Heavy cretonne, madras, muslin and quilts. For stitching aprons and men's work shirts. For making buttonholes.	40 to 60 Cotton C Silk Twist
18	Bed ticking, awnings, porch furniture covers, boy's duck suits.	30 to 40 Cotton D Silk Twist
19	Heavy weaves of coating, suiting, ticking, sacking, tarpaulin, duck, drilling, canvas. For wash uniforms and bedding supplies for hospitals and hotels.	24 to 30 Cotton E Silk Twist 60 to 80 Linen
21	Bags, Coarse Cloths and heavy Goods.	40 to 60 Linen or very Coarse Cotton

When sending orders for needles be sure to specify the size required.

You will obtain the best stitching results from your sewing machine if it is fitted with a Singer needle.

The Sign of

Singer Service

SINGER SEWING MACHINES

Throughout the World

SINGER SEWING LIBRARY — NO. 2

HOW TO MAKE

DRESSES

The Modern Singer Way

Published by Singer Sewing Machine Co., Inc.

FOREWORD

*W*OMAN'S creative instinct and love of beautiful things constantly tempt her to make for herself the many kinds of dresses called for by the modern wardrobe. Whether it be a simple morning dress, a dainty afternoon frock or a stately evening gown, all are possible with style, economy and little effort through the use of the Singer Sewing Machine and Singer short cut methods.

Dressmaking methods have been tremendously improved in recent years, so that the construction of a dress need no longer be laborious, time consuming or uncertain of result. All the newest methods, some of which have never before been published, have been gathered together in this book, in the simplest possible form for quick and easy reference.

With a modern Singer machine and this book, the making of lovely dresses becomes an easy, delightful accomplishment. When you have a modern Singer you know that you have in your home the finest machine that eighty-one years of progress have produced. And when you use the methods presented here you know that you are following the best practice that dressmaking experience has developed. If you need help in a particular problem, call at the nearest Singer Shop. They will gladly assist you.

Complete reference index on page 48

Published by

SINGER SEWING MACHINE CO., INC.

SINGER BUILDING, NEW YORK

Price 25 cents

How to make Dresses the

MODERN SINGER WAY

MAKING a dress should be a delightful adventure—never a tedious task, but a fascinating pastime. And it will be for you if you have the proper equipment and you proceed by the simple step-by-step method set forth in this book.

First you should know exactly what you are to do. Here are the eleven steps, you will find full and clear directions for each one in the pages that follow:

Step One—Decide upon the type of dress you want, its purpose, line, texture and color. Look through the fashion books. See what is being shown in the smart shops. Decide what style your dress shall be. Then buy a pattern as nearly like your ideal dress as you can, or adapt a simple pattern to your needs.

Step Two—Purchase your material, thread and trimming. To avoid waste, buy only the amount of material called for on the envelope of the pattern you are using. Buy also any notions that will be needed.

Step Three—Test and alter the pattern according to personal measurement chart. In the Singer Short Courses, free to the public, the use of this measurement chart is thoroughly explained.

Step Four—Read the instructions accompanying your pattern. Cut your dress with great care so that the grain and design run correctly and all parts are in accord. Notch and mark each part for assembling, not forgetting the under piece when material is doubled.

Step Five—Sit at your machine and see that it is in perfect condition; the stitch and tension adjusted, the needle in place, and all ready to sew.

Step Six—Do any tucking, gathering, plaiting, or shirring that is to come inside the foundation seams.

Step Seven—Use the sewing machine attachments to make any interesting trimming features.

Step Eight—Pin the shoulder and under-arm seams and baste them by machine for fitting.

Step Nine—Try the dress on and make any adjustments necessary to make it fit perfectly.

Step Ten—Stitch all the seams permanently and finish them on your machine. Remove bastings.

Step Eleven—Press all seams and joinings carefully. Finally press the dress, going over the seams as well as the material itself.

And now your dress is finished, ready to be worn the more proudly because you have made it all yourself.

I

Dressmaking Equipment

THE first essential to sewing is a good sewing machine. For the modern way to sew is by machine. With a modern Singer and Singer attachments, you have the means of stitching perfectly every type of fabric, making every type of seam and all the finishes called for in modern dressmaking more quickly, more easily and more perfectly than by hand. If you have electricity in your home, by all means investigate the time and labor saving advantages of an electric sewing machine.

It is not the purpose of this book to tell you how to operate and care for your sewing machine. The instruction book gives these directions fully. Read them carefully. Refer to them frequently.

Full instructions for using the attachments are contained in the book "Short Cuts to Home Sewing," a copy of which you should have. If desired, personal instructions may be obtained by calling at the nearest Singer Shop.

Whatever type of machine you have, make yourself thoroughly familiar with it. Find out where and how to oil it, how to set the needle correctly, how to wind the bobbin, and how to sit in an easy position at the machine.

The correct position at the machine is with the eyes straight in line with the presser foot, chair pulled close to the machine and absolutely square with it. Do not bend over the machine, but sit up to it.

If you are just beginning to sew by machine, draw lines with a ruler on a piece of paper or fabric and practice stitching along these lines. Practice making square and triangle forms, turning corners squarely, and keeping the rows straight and at even distances apart.

If you sit quietly at the sewing machine, sew with an even speed and guide the material easily under the presser foot, you will find that you have a straight seam, naturally. If you sit too far back from the machine, or huddle yourself up over it, or sew with nervous haste, you will rarely get a perfect seam. Sewing is a deliberate and enjoyable undertaking and should be so considered from the first to the last stitch.

Before stitching a seam, make a test seam on a scrap of the same material to see that the length of the stitch is as you desire, that the tension is right for a beautiful stitch and that thread and needle are in accord. See the Needle and Thread Chart on the inside back cover.

Have a pair of seven inch shears of good quality and keep them sharp for the sole purpose of cutting fabrics. Also have a pair of sharp pointed scissors at the machine for clipping threads and trimming seams.

You should have a thimble, sewing needles, tailor's chalk, tape, yardstick or four foot rule, and a smaller six-inch rule, this small rule to be kept on the machine for measuring hem widths and spacings.

An ironing board, sleeve board and iron are essential and should be conveniently near the sewing machine when you are sewing.

If much sewing is done on wool and velvet, you should have a velvet or needle press board. Such a board has a surface of very fine short wire bristles, like a stiff brush. On this surface you can press nap fabrics without pressing the nap down.

A drawer, box or basket should be provided for supplies and materials. There should be bias binding, seaming ribbon, tapes, cable cords in various sizes, threads (silk, cotton and embroidery), fasteners, buttons, elastic and all the convenient notions that save time in sewing.

A chalk marker that may be attached to a yard stick, machine leg, or door edge, for measuring and marking the length of your garment and a dependable pinking machine for finishing certain seams should be available.

There should be instruction and fashion books nearby when one is sewing, both for reference and inspiration. A different method of finishing a seam, a pocket or an edge, often adds interest and frequently saves time or makes for better or more satisfactory work. It pays to learn the newest and best way. Correct methods, good equipment and enthusiasm make sewing really enjoyable.

3

Machine Made Seams

SEAMS are as important in providing beauty in garments, as they are essential to the shaping of them. Expensive frocks are always interestingly cut and beautifully seamed.

In making seams the object is to join two pieces of material together by easy, perfectly lined stitching that varies not a hair's width in its course. The pieces should be so accurately joined, without drawing or pulling, that they appear as though grown together.

The seams shown here are termed Essential Seams. Some are as old as sewing. Some originated with the sewing machine. Skill in making the seams, as well as knowing where and when to use them is necessary for professional appearing work. Seams should be elastic, never tight.

Use thread of an appropriate size for the fabric, needles right in size for the thread and a stitch right in length for all.

Always begin a seam at the top and stitch down. For instance, begin at

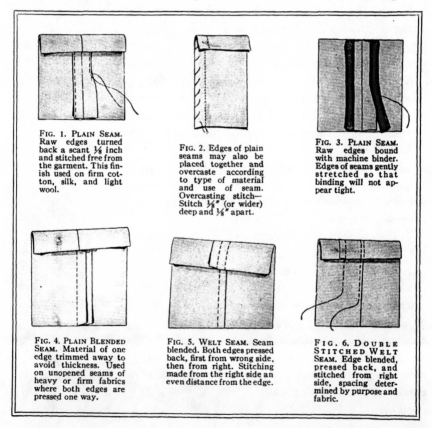

FIG. 1. PLAIN SEAM. Raw edges turned back a scant ⅛ inch and stitched free from the garment. This finish used on firm cotton, silk, and light wool.

FIG. 2. Edges of plain seams may also be placed together and overcaste according to type of material and use of seam. Overcasting stitch— Stitch ⅛" (or wider) deep and ⅛" apart.

FIG. 3. PLAIN SEAM. Raw edges bound with machine binder. Edges of seams gently stretched so that binding will not appear tight.

FIG. 4. PLAIN BLENDED SEAM. Material of one edge trimmed away to avoid thickness. Used on unopened seams of heavy or firm fabrics where both edges are pressed one way.

FIG. 5. WELT SEAM. Seam blended. Both edges pressed back, first from wrong side, then from right. Stitching made from the right side an even distance from the edge.

FIG. 6. DOUBLE STITCHED WELT SEAM. Edge blended, pressed back, and stitched from right side, spacing determined by purpose and fabric.

the neck for the shoulder seam; begin at the armhole for the under-arm and sleeve seams.

To make beautiful seams, have your machine in perfect order, oiled and wiped clean of surplus oil. A straight, unblunted needle is necessary to good work. Thread of the same kind and number should be used on top and in the bobbin, which must be evenly wound.

The two edges that are to be sewed should be laid together on a flat surface, bringing them together across the fabric, rather than lengthwise. This avoids stretching. With last three fingers of the right hand push the edges together just as you would shift one sheet of paper over another. Pin the seam every few inches, placing the pins crosswise on the seam.

When making joining seams, such as in the widths of a skirt, stitch them up at once. In making fitting seams, as at shoulder and under-arm, baste the edges together on the machine. For machine basting, use the longest stitch possible and number 80 cotton thread in white or black. After a garment is fitted stitch inside or outside the basting line, as the garment requires, and then remove basting.

Finish the edges of bound or edge-stitched seams before pressing them. Always press a seam before it is joined to another.

FIG. 7. TUCK OR OPEN WELT. Same as a Welt Seam, except inside seam edge is blended only 1/16 inch. First row of stitching put in as basting and removed.

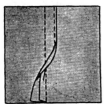

FIG. 8. FLAT FELLED SEAM. One edge blended free edge turned in ⅛ inch and stitched on right side. Use for tailored wash garments requiring sturdy seams.

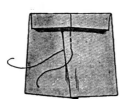

FIG. 9. FRENCH SEAM. Particularly desirable for sheer fabrics, for lingerie and children's dresses. May be used in fine and light weight materials where a flat seam is not essential. It varies in width from a scant ⅛ inch to ¼ inch. Usually made by first making a ⅛ inch seam on the right side, then trimming the raw edges evenly, creasing the seam and stitching ¼ inch from the edge on the wrong side, which conceals completely the first seam and all raw edges.

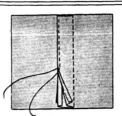

FIG. 10. PLAIN SEAM, with edges turned inside and stitched together. Used on garments of sheer or light weight material that are closely fitted and require a sturdy seam.

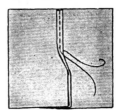

FIG. 11. HEMMED SEAM. In joining the seam one edge is slipped back a scant ¼ inch. The widest edge is put in the hemmer and hemmed down, one row of stitching holding all.

Stitching Fabrics

FINE woolen fabrics, gingham, lawn, or linen or cotton fabrics of firm, even weave, are very easy to handle in stitching and require no special precaution. But filmy fabrics or those of varying textures require different treatments in assembling seams or in passing under the presser foot so that the seams will always be even, elastic and smooth.

When stitching fabrics never allow the weight of the fabric to pull from the presser foot. Lift up any bulk of material so that its weight rests on the machine. Guide the material along the seam or stitching line. Never pull the material from the back. The stitch is thereby lengthened unevenly and stretched out of shape, and the beauty of the seam is lost. Forcing the feed may also bend or break the needle and damage parts of the stitching mechanism.

With needle and thread of the right kind and number and the tension and stitch properly adjusted to the texture of the fabric, a perfect seam should result. If the seam is not perfect, refer to "Short Cuts to Home Sewing," find out what the trouble is and correct it at once.

Stitching Silk Fabrics. Various types of silk, such as flat crepe, crepe de Chine, and satin, differ in their stitching qualities. Flat crepe, because of its firm, even weave, is usually the easiest of all to stitch.

Crepe de Chine, because of its variance in weight, being sometimes quite flimsy and other times heavy, requires care in placing together for seaming so that one edge will not draw more than the other. The seam should be adjusted with great care at the outset and pinned at frequent intervals along the seam line so that the fabric will not slip or draw more on one side than the other.

Satin has a tendency to slip in the seams, requiring vigilance in making and careful basting so that the seams will remain in position while stitching.

Brocades which vary in their thickness also require watching in passing under the presser foot so that the seam will be kept straight as the presser foot drops or rises from one thickness to another.

Stitching Lace, Chiffon and Georgette. A firm cotton lace can be stitched as a fabric. Filmy lace or fine texture has not sufficient weight to carry over the feed easily and therefore should be stitched over a piece of newspaper, or other paper that tears easily. The needle perforates the paper and causes it to pull away easily after the seam is finished.

In stitching chiffon and georgette, newspaper underneath the fabric will prevent tightening of the seam. Often French seams are made in these materials. The paper underneath helps to keep the narrow first seam even, and insures perfection for the second seam.

When preparing sheer materials for hemstitching or picoting, adjust the sewing machine for as long a stitch as you can, loosen the tension as you would for basting, and stitch over paper wherever you want the hemstitching or picoting to come, keeping the lines true and in correct position. Use the same thread for marking line for hemstitching as will be used for stitching the dress. The work can be done directly over this stitching line, thus insuring accuracy and avoiding stretching.

6

It also obviates the necessity of removing the bastings afterwards. The same precaution used in stitching lace, chiffon and georgette are observed.

Stitching Metallics. The warp thread in metallics is usually quite pronounced, the fabric raveling easily when cut on the cross or bias. Where the warp thread is heavier than the woof, lay the seams over paper while stitching. This prevents their pulling or slipping.

When making a curved seam in metallic cloth or chiffon velvet, lay the edge flat on a piece of paper, allow the seam to take its natural shape, the warp and woof threads parallel with the square edges of the paper, and stitch the curved edge just as it is. It will thus be true to shape in the finished garment. Metallic fabrics that fray should have the raw edges bound with seaming ribbon before they are joined.

Stitching Fur and Pile Fabrics. Because of their depth, loosen the tension, lengthen the stitch, and pin the two thicknesses of the seam together every few inches so that they will not slip.

Always stitch the way of the nap except in the case of erect pile velvet, which may be stitched against the nap. Use silk thread even when basting velvet fabrics, to avoid marking the fabric with the thread.

Stitching Wool Fabrics. Light weight wool is stitched the same as silk. For Coatings, it is necessary to lengthen the stitch. It is advisable also to allow generous seam widths in cutting.

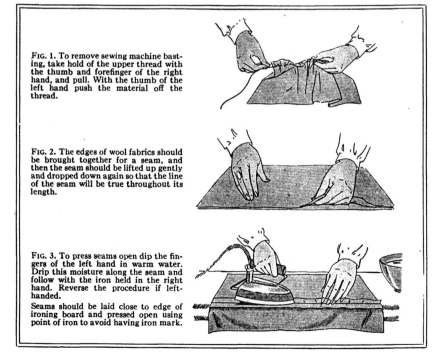

FIG. 1. To remove sewing machine basting, take hold of the upper thread with the thumb and forefinger of the right hand, and pull. With the thumb of the left hand push the material off the thread.

FIG. 2. The edges of wool fabrics should be brought together for a seam, and then the seam should be lifted up gently and dropped down again so that the line of the seam will be true throughout its length.

FIG. 3. To press seams open dip the fingers of the left hand in warm water. Drip this moisture along the seam and follow with the iron held in the right hand. Reverse the procedure if left-handed.

Seams should be laid close to edge of ironing board and pressed open using point of iron to avoid having iron mark.

Style and Fabric Selection

EVERY woman can be fashionably and becomingly dressed if she is alert to the sources of style formation. The fashion magazines, the shop windows advertisements of smart ready to wear, photos of what smart women are wearing and clothes you see worn by well dressed women, all can be drawn upon for ideas for your own wardrobe.

When selecting a style, be guided first by the purpose of the dress, and second by the time at your disposal to make it. In other words, if a dress must be made in an afternoon or in an evening, or in a day at the most, do not select a design that calls for elaborate stitching and intricate details, but choose a simple style that you know is becoming and practical for the purpose.

The number of dresses in your wardrobe, the season's becoming colors, whether the costume is to be worn for afternoon, for evening, for business or for traveling —all these points should be taken into consideration so that the dress will accord in every way with its purpose. Truly artistic clothes are designed for a purpose, and in line, color, texture and finish, meet their requirements adequately.

In selecting a style for a dress, do not be satisfied with what you find in one fashion magazine, rather look through several, so as to judge the popular necklines, sleeve and skirt effects and determine which of those favored will be most becoming and serve you most satisfactorily in every way. Then choose a pattern that most nearly comes up to the ideal of the frock you have in mind. Do not allow yourself to be prejudiced by the color or fabric illustrated in the fashion magazine, but try to see the lines of the garment and how it will appear in the fabric you intend to use.

In selecting the fabrics, cost, utility and effect must be considered. Woolen materials can be bought at from one to fifteen dollars a yard. If you are to have two wool frocks in a season, then it would be better to buy the higher grade fabrics. Such fabrics will be of a quality that will allow them to be worn frequently and bear the cleaning and pressing necessary for service frocks.

In summer, when a variety of clothes is desirable, it is better to buy less expensive fabrics, such as flannel, wool crepe, wash silks, and smart cotton or linen materials. In this way you can afford to have a greater number of frocks and can distribute the work of making as your time allows.

In buying silks, it is better to buy a $2.50 flat crepe than a $2.50 satin, because the flat crepe at that price will give more service and look nice for a longer time than the satin.

It is better to buy a very good quality cotton frock than a cheap silk one, because of the ser-

8

vice and beauty that are to be had from the best quality of the one fabric as against the cheap quality of the other.

Avoid using flimsy materials for tailored frocks, or heavy materials for frocks that call for voile, georgette or chiffon. The effect in the finished dress is important, and the fabric and design must be in accord if a harmonious dress is to result.

Your Type. To make successful clothes for yourself, determine first your type. If you are over-tall, avoid dresses that exaggerate your height; if short, avoid dresses that emphasize your shortness, and so on. Further details may be obtained at the nearest Singer Shop.

The safest way is to always buy the pattern first. The pattern envelope will tell how much material is required according to size of pattern and width of material. However, patterns may not be near by and time may be limited, thereby making it inconvenient to choose the pattern first. Under the circumstances the following old time rule may help, bearing in mind that some of the present day styles require more yardage than the average straight simple dress. In the case of material 36 or 40 inches wide, measure twice the length of the figure from shoulder to the desired skirt, plus one yard for sleeves and hem finish.

Clothes' Becomingness. Dresses designed as mere coverings are never modish and rarely becoming. A dress should express in color, texture and line something of the quality of mind and good taste of the wearer if the garment is to be complimentary to her. A dress can rarely be smart that is not first becoming. A woman who lacks natural style sense would do better to make certain that the dress is becoming rather than to seek to express fashion's most extreme style.

Estimating Material Requirements. Often when shopping, you see just the material you would like to have for a dress. The question of quantity to buy is always a problem, particularly if the material is expensive. For a plaited or circular skirt an additional skirt length should be added, or ¾ to one yard more. For a dress with a plaited or circular skirt, use 4½ yards. A plaited skirt alone requires in width three times the hip measurement, plus ¼ yard for finishing.

The average sleeveless waist lining requires one yard of 36-inch material if a seam is made at the back, or 1¼ yards if the seam is omitted.

The average coat or wool frock of 54-inch fabric requires two lengths from shoulder to floor.

Dresses of 32-inch material usually require three lengths from shoulder to desired skirt length for a figure larger than 36-inch bust. Smaller sizes require only two lengths plus one yard for sleeves and hem finish.

9

Handling Fabrics

ONE of the first essentials to overcoming an amateurish look in a garment is to press it thoroughly as the garment is being constructed. Every seam and part as it joins another should be carefully pressed. When the garment is completed, press it again.

Learn to join seams and apply sections so that they will not need to be stretched into position, but remember also the value of the iron and of cautious steaming to give a new frock the professionally finished look.

Tailors who press men's clothes will, for a very small fee, press a wool dress or coat that has been made at home. Often it is well to take such garments to the tailor and see how the pressing is done. This will give you assurance, as well as show you the care that is used.

Different fabrics require different methods of sponging and pressing. Taffeta should never have water applied to it, nor be pressed with a hot iron.

Rayon requires a dry cloth over it and an iron that is not too hot. If in pressing rayon or taffeta a very firm pressing is found to be necessary, then prepare to steam the fabric by putting a dry cloth over the fabric and another cloth that has been wrung as dry as possible over the dry cloth, and press, using a hotter iron than when pressing direct.

There is a distinct difference between ironing and pressing. In pressing, the iron is lifted gently over the fabric. In ironing, one irons out with strength and firmness, not only smoothing out all the wrinkles, but at the same time restoring the shape of the garment.

During the making of a cotton or linen garment, a moderate iron may be used on the fabric itself. Press on the wrong side. Then for the final pressing, use a thin cloth that has been wrung as dry as possible from warm water and press thoroughly from the right side, with the cloth between the dress and the iron.

For wool, a heavy muslin press cloth should be used. This should be dipped in almost hot water and wrung as dry as possible. Woolen fabrics require more pressure than others, but in no case should an ironing motion be employed.

In pressing seams in fabrics that mark easily, slip strips of paper under the seam edges, moving them along under the seam as you press. This will prevent the seam's width from showing through on the right side.

Velvets and pile fabrics should be steamed or pressed over a velvet pressboard. When a board is used, pressing must be done from the wrong side, using a dry cloth over the fabric. Rarely is moisture necessary. When it is used, two cloths are required, a dry one next to the fabric with a damp one next to the iron. A wire brush usually accompanies a wire pressboard, this to lift the nap in fabric and to aid in restoring the pile of fabrics that have been pressed under too much moisture.

In steaming fabrics with a damp cloth over a hot iron, have sufficient cloth over the iron so that the steam will filter through and not be wet when it reaches the fabric, but just damp enough to be effective. Hold material with wrong side next to steam and brush nap the way it runs. Use a fine, soft, clean brush with the steaming—a wire one or a whisk broom on heavy fabrics.

Using Patterns

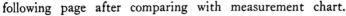

THE modern pattern, with its printed instructions for use, has greatly simplified dressmaking. It provides a means by which you can select a smart design and secure at little cost a safe, economical, and illuminating guide for developing it.

As a general rule when a new design is created by a pattern manufacturer, it is first developed in size 16. Other sizes are then graded up and down throughout the range of measurements from the master pattern. Allowance is made on all patterns for style fullness.

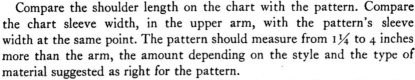

Buy your pattern according to bust measurement, using snug measurement if you prefer close-fitting clothes; easy, if otherwise. Alter pattern for irregularities as suggested on the following page after comparing with measurement chart.

Compare the shoulder length on the chart with the pattern. Compare the chart sleeve width, in the upper arm, with the pattern's sleeve width at the same point. The pattern should measure from 1¼ to 4 inches more than the arm, the amount depending on the style and the type of material suggested as right for the pattern.

Tie a tape around the figure at a becoming waist line and lengthen or shorten the pattern of the skirt and the waist to bring these sections in accordance with the waist line position that you have decided upon.

Test the pattern carefully so that it corresponds with the measurements of the individual. Then cut the dress by the altered pattern.

When making pattern alterations make them inside the pattern rather than on the edges so that the pattern will retain its original outlines.

The pattern alterations shown take care of the average corrections. No figure requires all the alterations given here. Often none are needed, and in any event one or two alterations usually prove sufficient.

Selecting and Altering Patterns

THE normal figure is from five feet five inches to five feet seven inches in height, and has a hip measurement three inches larger than the bust measurement. A woman of such proportions can buy an average pattern in the bust size and have very little change to make to have it fit perfectly. A few precautions are given here that will help in selecting patterns for types that vary from the average.

For the Slight Mature Figure. Buy a junior size pattern. Note the measurements on the pattern envelope and be guided by these rather than by the age specified. There are always one and two-piece junior dress patterns that vary little in silhouette from adult patterns, but the pattern itself is more nearly in accordance with the proper size than the larger pattern. A mature appearance will be given the junior pattern through the color of the fabric and the fitting and finish of the dress.

For the Small, Well Developed Figure. Buy either a junior or average pattern, and shorten in waist and skirt and sleeve, reducing the trimming pieces as well as the foundation pieces of the pattern.

For the Figure with Full Back at Neck and Hips. Buy a pattern one size larger than the bust measurement, put darts in the front shoulders, and tucks at the back neck. An open revere collar is best for such types, especially when the neck is large.

For the Figure with High Shoulders. Use a regular pattern and cut the shoulder seams one-half inch higher at armhole edge, or cut wider seams at the shoulders, and fit as required.

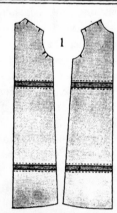 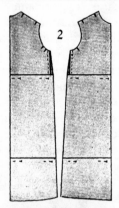 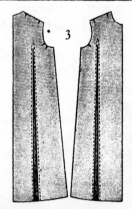

FIG. 1. TO LENGTHEN A PATTERN. Slash above and below waist. Place strips of paper under, separating pattern to desired length. Pin paper in place. Check length by measuring; then replace pins with stitching.

FIG. 2. TO SHORTEN A PATTERN. Lay folds above and below waist line. Place pieces of paper at under-arms to true the seam. If hem is allowed for, indicate it on the pattern. Side seams should measure the same.

FIG. 3. LARGER HIPS THAN BUST. Slash pattern front and back. Separate as shown, enough to measure 4 inches more (plus seams) than the figure measures around the fullest part of the hips.

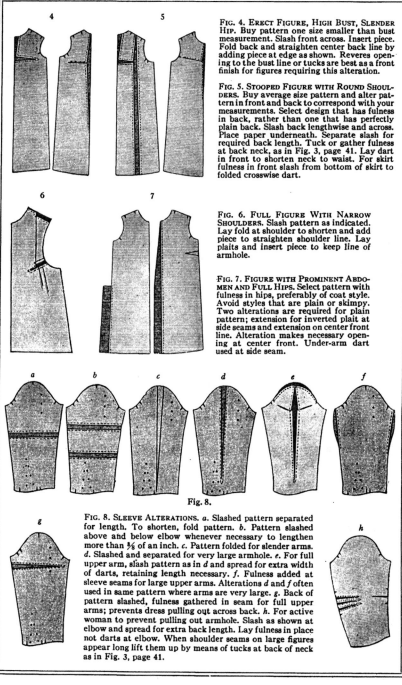

FIG. 4. ERECT FIGURE, HIGH BUST, SLENDER HIP. Buy pattern one size smaller than bust measurement. Slash front across. Insert piece. Fold back and straighten center back line by adding piece at edge as shown. Reveres opening to the bust line or tucks are best as a front finish for figures requiring this alteration.

FIG. 5. STOOPED FIGURE WITH ROUND SHOULDERS. Buy average size pattern and alter pattern in front and back to correspond with your measurements. Select design that has fulness in back, rather than one that has perfectly plain back. Slash back lengthwise and across. Place paper underneath. Separate slash for required back length. Tuck or gather fulness at back neck, as in Fig. 3, page 41. Lay dart in front to shorten neck to waist. For skirt fulness in front slash from bottom of skirt to folded crosswise dart.

FIG. 6. FULL FIGURE WITH NARROW SHOULDERS. Slash pattern as indicated. Lay fold at shoulder to shorten and add piece to straighten shoulder line. Lay plaits and insert piece to keep line of armhole.

FIG. 7. FIGURE WITH PROMINENT ABDOMEN AND FULL HIPS. Select pattern with fulness in hips, preferably of coat style. Avoid styles that are plain or skimpy. Two alterations are required for plain pattern; extension for inverted plait at side seams and extension on center front line. Alteration makes necessary opening at center front. Under-arm dart used at side seam.

Fig. 8.

FIG. 8. SLEEVE ALTERATIONS. a. Slashed pattern separated for length. To shorten, fold pattern. b. Pattern slashed above and below elbow whenever necessary to lengthen more than ⅜ of an inch. c. Pattern folded for slender arms. d. Slashed and separated for very large armhole. e. For full upper arm, slash pattern as in d and spread for extra width of darts, retaining length necessary. f. Fulness added at sleeve seams for large upper arms. Alterations d and f often used in same pattern where arms are very large. g. Back of pattern slashed, fulness gathered in seam for full upper arms; prevents dress pulling out across back. h. For active woman to prevent pulling out armhole. Slash as shown at elbow and spread for extra back length. Lay fulness in place not darts at elbow. When shoulder seams on large figures appear long lift them up by means of tucks at back of neck as in Fig. 3, page 41.

Cutting Out a Dress

BEFORE placing the pattern on the material, straighten one end of the fabric. To do this, clip the selvage and tear across quickly, or pull a thread and cut on the pulled thread line. Most fabrics tear satisfactorily except corded fabrics, heavy linens and metallics. All plain non-corded fabrics, or those with a design woven in, such as gingham or yarn dyed cotton, linen, silks, woolens and velvet can be straightened in this way.

Place the pattern on the material from the straightened end. Pin the selvages together from the straightened end, or open the material out, as the pattern layout requires.

Printed material often causes difficulty because the printing is not "straight with the goods," that is, in line with the woof of the fabric. When buying printed fabrics it is always well to notice whether or not it is printed straight and avoid pieces that are visibly printed off grain. A dress that is not cut with the grain of the fabric will never set well and will not be as attractive when worn. A dress of printed material that is not cut with the design will be equally unattractive. Therefore be cautious in buying the fabric at the outset.

Always cut materials with the grain. For instance, in a dress that has ruffles, use the pattern piece simply to determine the width and length to make the ruffles, but tear the fabric or pull a thread, rather than cut by the pattern.

For true bias ruffles it is better to determine from the pattern the width desired and then with the yard stick mark true bias lines of the required width, cutting on the lines rather than using the pattern.

The same is true of straight belts, bands, and folds. Let the pattern tell you how wide and long to cut them and then cut them on the lengthwise or crosswise or true bias.

When cutting chiffon, georgette, transparent velvet, or any material that creeps and is difficult to handle take the precaution to pin all corners to the table, using thumb tacks or pins.

When you are ready to place the fabric, open up the pattern envelope and separate the pieces, laying the trimming pieces to one side. Read carefully the instructions accompanying the pattern. Measure the length of the pattern pieces and make any necessary alterations according to the measurement chart.

Place the pattern on the material according to the layout chart furnished with the pattern. Pin the pieces accurately to position, using plenty of pins to hold the pattern to the cloth. If the material is double be sure that the grain is true both at top and bottom. As a precaution, measure with a tape from the straight edge in to the first and last of the group of three large perforations to make sure that these are straight with the grain.

Use the shears in cutting and make long swaths so that the seam edge will be even. Place one hand down on the material and keep the shears on the table while cutting. Do not lift the fabric up from the table as you cut.

To cut the notches, lift the fabric up and fold the edges together at the point where the notch comes. Then cut the notch with points extending out from edge of seam. Notches cut into the seam allowed may interfere with the seam line and cause dress to pull out at their points. Each notch may be marked with thread or chalk instead of cutting the material.

In the case of materials that fray easily, always cut a little outside the pattern edge for a deeper seam and mark the notches with chalk or thread.

When cutting collars, cuffs, bands and other trimming pieces, consider how they are to be finished. If the edges are to be bound or finished with applied bands, the seam allowance should be cut away from the pattern before it is placed on the material; otherwise they might appear larger than desired.

Mark the perforations where the darts, tucks or plaits come, with tailor's tacks, so that these may be placed accurately after the pattern has been removed.

Before removing the front and back pieces of the pattern, run a long, basting stitch in threads of contrasting color down the center front and center back lines of the garment. These serve as guides in fitting and should remain in place until the dress is finished.

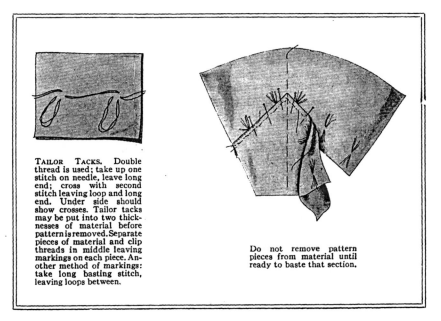

TAILOR TACKS. Double thread is used; take up one stitch on needle, leave long end; cross with second stitch leaving loop and long end. Under side should show crosses. Tailor tacks may be put into two thicknesses of material before pattern is removed. Separate pieces of material and clip threads in middle leaving markings on each piece. Another method of markings: take long basting stitch, leaving loops between.

Do not remove pattern pieces from material until ready to baste that section.

Assembling a One Piece Dress

A TYPICAL one-piece dress has been selected as the first to be described in this book. When the making of this dress is perfectly understood any simple dress can be undertaken with success.

When assembling a simple garment such as this, basting may be omitted or machine basting used. Hand basting is required only when there are many intricate shapings, or square points, or circular lines, or applied sections calling for top stitching, when the material is sheer or limp.

When preparing a one-piece dress for fitting, first space pin and stitch the tucks or darts in the front shoulders. In joining the shoulder seams place the pins crosswise, adjusting the fullness so that it comes in the center of the shoulder. Join the front and back shoulder pieces so that there is no jog in the neck line or armhole line. The back shoulder line of the dress is usually ½ inch longer than the front. This allows a slight stretching in the front and ease in the back which cause the dress to fit perfectly in the hollow of the front shoulder and to be comfortable over the full part of the shoulder blades. Stitch the shoulder seams, beginning at the neck.

Stitch the under-arm seams, stitching from the armhole down, and removing the pins as you approach them in the seam. Pin the sleeves from both top and bottom, toward the center, easing in the elbow fullness between the notches. Sew the sleeve seams, stitching from the armhole down. Run machine basting from notch to notch across the top of the sleeve. Draw up the thread and place the sleeves in the armhole, holding the sleeve toward you, all notches to position. When the sleeves are pinned in place, look to see that the lengthwise grain in the sleeve hangs directly down from the top of the shoulder. Adjust the sleeves if necessary and baste them in, using the machine basting stitch.

Measure the length of the dress from the shoulder at the neck to the bottom. Turn the hem and pin it in place. When a hem has been first turned up and pinned it is much easier to test the dress for length in fitting. The effect of the dress is also more readily obtained.

To make sure that the neck is cut large enough to slip over the head, the neck of the dress should measure two inches more than the head so that it can be slipped on and off easily. It is desirable to place a row of machine basting around the neck to keep the edge from stretching. If it is preferred not to trim the neck until after fitting, open the left shoulder seam two or three inches to allow the dress to slip on easily.

Fitting the Dress. When putting the dress on for fitting always take hold of it at the shoulders and square it up on the figure, lifting the seams to the same position on each shoulder. Be sure that the dress is rightly adjusted before you start to fit it.

The shoulder and armhole lines are of first importance. They should fit smoothly, without a wrinkle. Observe the darts and see whether they are deep or long or short enough. Has the fulness been eased in sufficiently at the back shoulder? Is the end of the shoulder line at a becoming point? Could the fitting of the neck be improved if it were trimmed slightly at the sides? Would it be more becoming if it were cut a little lower at the center front?

Consider all these points carefully. Notice the position of the sleeve. Does it need to be moved backward or forward? Does the grain of the sleeve hang straight down from the shoulder seam? If there is any variation in the size of the arms, fit both sleeves.

Turn the sleeve up at the bottom for the proper length. Always bend the arm up toward the chest in determining the length of the sleeve so as to be sure that the sleeve is sufficiently long from the elbow to the wrist.

Pin the belt on at a becoming line. If the belt itself has not been made ready, use a tape for this and pin it so that the size and location will be correct for finishing. Never place pockets or determine a hem line until the belt has been taken care of, that is, in a dress that has a belt. The belt shortens the dress at least one inch because it holds the dress in.

Place the pockets to position and notice whether or not they are at a becoming distance apart. Sometimes to bring them a little closer than the perforations indicate will make the figure appear smaller through the hips, or if placed farther apart the hips may appear wider. Consider this in placing them on. Their size, both in width and length, also has something to do with the depth they are below the waist line.

After the dress has been finally fitted, consider the length of the dress and make sure it is even and the hem is at a becoming point.

  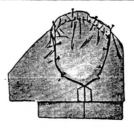

a b

FIG. 1. (a) STITCHING DARTS. Measure and stitch both darts the same depth. Begin at the top and stitch down, tapering the dart to a shallow point at the lower end or leave ends long enough to tie three times, reversing thread each time to form a square knot. Leave ends at least $\frac{1}{2}$ inch long when cut off.

(b) Darts can also be made by threading bobbin thread up through the eye of the needle in a direction opposite to that in which the upper thread is drawn, then tie bobbin thread to upper thread and pull up through tension discs. Stitching is started at point of dart and in this way no thread ends are visible at the point of dart.

FIG. 3. PUTTING THE SLEEVES IN. Run a row of machine basting between the notches, within the seam allowance. Place notch at top of sleeve even with shoulder seam, other notches meeting. Hold sleeve toward you. Place pins as shown and adjust fulness between the notches. Lengthwise center of sleeve must hang straight down from tip of shoulder. Any shoulder or underarm alteration makes necessary corresponding sleeve adjustment.

FIG. 2. FINISHING DARTS. Darts more than $\frac{1}{8}$ inch wide at the top should be slashed to within 2 inches of the end and opened out flat as in Fig. 2. Overcast the raw edges as shown but do not draw the overcasting tight. Press the dart from the top down.

Finishing a One Piece Dress

WHEN the fitting is considered complete in a dress, stand away from mirror enough to notice all parts carefully and see if any improvements can be made. Then go over the pins and adjust them so that when the dress is removed there will be no variation in them and no doubts as to where the alterations should be made. If there is any variation in height of the shoulders or length or fullness of arms, take the precaution to fit both sides.

When the dress is removed mark all alterations so that they can be made perfectly and without marring in any way the contour of the seams.

Measure the neck edge of the dress and measure the head. The dress should be at least two inches larger than the head so that it will slip on and off easily.

Stitch all foundation seams finally. Finish the raw edges in accordance with the approved method for the fabric used. Here a pinking machine will be found practical, but it should never be used on fabrics that fray easily. Remove all bastings and press seams. When pressing the sleeve seams, use a sleeve board or rolling pin covered with a towel so that no creases will form in the sleeve. Press the armhole seams in toward the dress.

Finish the cuffs and neck of the dress according to pattern and vogue. If binding is used, finish the joinings or ends of the binding neatly in each part. If as large an opening is desired for the head as the bound neck allows, take especial care in putting the binding on so that the neck will not be drawn smaller than it measures before finishing. If a still larger opening is desired for the head, open the left shoulder seam to the dart and bind the seam with seaming ribbon so that a flat finish will result. Use two small snap fasteners or hooks with flat eyes for the opening; make the opening before binding the neck.

When patch pockets are applied, turn the corners at the bottom by lifting the presser foot when the exact point is reached and pivoting the material on the needle, turning it around so that an exact point will be made at the bottom of the pocket. Pivoting in this way is necessary on all corners or points where perfect stitching is the aim.

Make the hem at the bottom of the dress, using the method described on pages 20 and 21 that is best suited to the fabric.

Make the belt and side seam straps as explained in detail in pattern instructions. Finish the end of the belt with a tailored bow or slide buckle, or join it in a plain seam and conceal the seam under the strap at the side seam.

Variations for a One Piece Dress. Every season fashion offers one-piece dresses in a variety of styles. They may have plaits, tiers or flounces, or they may have bands stitched on the skirt to give weight and trimming. They may have peasant or plain sleeves, and the collar line may be high or low, square or V, as the fashion itself decrees.

In this book you will find many suggestions for finishing waist lines and neck and hem lines. All suggestions are applicable to a foundation dress. When you have become thoroughly familiar with the details in this book you will be able to use any of them at will to make any finishes that fashion may approve. Be on the alert for new methods of finishing because in the finishing or trimming features we find the most pronounced style changes. The silhouette of a frock changes only gradually. The fabric used, and the trimming, whether it is contrasting or harmonizing, whether it is a different fabric from the dress or of the dress fabric itself, speaks more for the style of the garment than the shaping does. Therefore, watch for the changes in trimming and finishing features so that your dress will express the newest features and be in every way in step with the mode.

The skill in making garments which in style and craftsmanship rival those of professionals, makes a delight of sewing. To achieve this desired goal, see good fashions and always copy from the best, not the cheapest. Cheap dresses made with the idea of speed only are not examples to follow in making distinctive clothes.

Learn first to assemble garments perfectly and then to make the narrowest bindings, the flattest and most perfect hems, to stitch and press turns so that they are perfect in form, and to finish pockets, make dainty collar and cuff finishes so that they will express enviable perfection. The width of a hem and its finish can make or destroy the style of a dress.

Your choice of the kind and width of seams and finishes will make for daintiness or clumsiness. Perfection comes in this from observation and practice.

Your machine will respond to your will, and it is your intelligence and experience that will be reflected in the garments you make, particularly in the finishes that mark good workmanship.

A   B

FIG. 1. SLEEVE FINISH. Cut bias strip, turn one edge and stitch down once. Stitch other edge to sleeve, placing right sides together as in A. Mitre corners, turn inside, press and slip stitch edge to sleeve—B.

FIG. 3. APPLYING PATCH POCKETS. Turn the edges of the pocket. Turn the ends of the binding in and stitch it to place across the top. At the ends clip away any surplus turns in the seams necessary to make a flat finish. See also Welt pockets, page 34.

FIG. 2. SIDE SEAM PLAITS. Finish the seam edges of the dress. Fold the inverted plait to position as shown. Clip the side seam. Stitch the plaits in a seam across the top, whip the raw edges or turn them in and stitch across. If a belt covers the top of the plaits stitching may extend through to right side of dress. Above plaits desirable for "full hip" figures.

Turning and Finishing Hems

MOST dresses have a hem or a foundation hem line an even distance from the floor all around. Occasionally uneven hems are fashionable. When used, they should be hung with special care for becomingness.

In preparing a dress for fitting, measure with a tape the approximate finished length, turn the hem to the wrong side, and pin it, with pin heads up, every eight or ten inches all the way around. If a belt is to be worn with the dress, tie a tape around the figure at a becoming waist line, and then, standing before the mirror, decide from the front what the becoming skirt length is. If it should be longer or shorter, adjust the pins.

A dress which hangs evenly at the bottom when worn varies in actual length at front, back and sides because of the shape of the figure. But all the variation comes between the natural waist line and the fullest part of the hip. An even hem measures exactly the same from the fullest part of the hip to the bottom all the way around.

The simplest of many ways to even the hem line is to hold a yard stick up to the figure. Note at the fullest part of the hip the distance from the floor, and keeping a finger at this point on the yard stick, move it around the figure, placing pins parallel with the floor. It is usually advisable to have another person place the pins across the back, or a chalk marker attached to a yard stick or the table leg of your sewing machine at the desired position may be used.

When the pins are in place remove the dress and place it flat on the work table. Fold it at the center front and center back. Measure from the pin line down to the point that has been decided upon as the becoming length. Make the hem even, measuring the same distance from the pin line all the way around.

If the material is firm, the hem may be creased and its depth measured for evenness. Dresses made of flimsy or limp material, because of the many pins required to hold it, may need to be put on a second time in order to make sure that there is no sag.

In making a circular skirt, take an extra precaution by hanging it up for at least twenty-four hours to allow the circular part to drop down and sag as much as it will. This will prevent sagging after the skirt is finished.

Finishing Hems. When the hem is even, measure its depth, using for this a piece of cardboard that has a notch cut in it for the width of the hem at its narrowest point. Lay the garment out on the table and run the cardboard marker all around the hem, marking with chalk or pins in line with the marked notch. Then if there is any flare in the skirt, run a machine basting one-quarter inch below the row of marks, stitching in the free edge of the hem only. In this way the basting can be drawn up as a gathering thread to insure an even distribution of the fulness. Trim the hem on the marked line and proceed to finish according to the most suitable method from the standpoint of style and fabric.

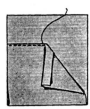

FIG. 1. PLAIN HEM. Edge turned, stitching showing on right side. Used generally for household sewing and children's clothes. Often several parallel rows of stitching are made directly under the first row as trimming for tailored frocks.

FIG. 2. SLIPSTITCHED HEM. Used where no stitching is to show on right side. Hem edge is first stitched and slipstitches taken in this edge, deeper, firmer stitches in edge than in dress. Back stitch taken in stitched edge every six or eight stitches. Thread not drawn tight.

FIG. 3. CIRCULAR HEM. Machine basting thread drawn up to control fulness and to allow even adjustment. Raw edge bound or covered with seaming ribbon, as in Fig. 4. Finished edge may be slipstitched or machine stitched to place. Where a skirt is very circular it is advisable to cut a facing the same shape as bottom of skirt and face as Fig. 2, page 32.

FIG. 4. PLAIT HEM. When plaits are creased on the seams it is necessary to clip the seam and press it open inside the hem, this for flatness and to prevent a ridge. Seaming ribbon is shown stitched correctly to position.

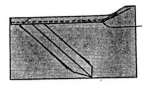

FIG. 5. NARROW HEM. Ruffles, bands and flounces are usually cut on a true bias and finished with a narrow hem made with the machine hemmer of a width that is in harmony with fabric and purpose. The manner of trimming the bias seam before it goes into the hemmer is shown, this to insure perfection.

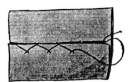

FIG. 6. CATCH STITCH HEM. Stitch from left to right. Pick up crosswise stitch on needle. Another crosswise ⅛ inch below and to right of first stitch, then another even with first stitch. Thread crosses itself.

Finishing Edges

THE sewing machine, with its hemming and binding attachments, is the perfect medium for edge finishes.

The type of finish to be used is often determined by the character of the fabric. Taffeta edges are most frequently hemmed or bound, georgette bound, voile or fine cotton hemmed or bound, organdie hemmed, linen bound. All may be picoted. A variance of the rule is often made so that a garment may be in keeping with a certain style. Fashion may bind or hem to be different, or for the sake of variety, so it is essential to know how to do both perfectly, since one or the other will invariably serve for the fabrics used.

Velvet and metallic edges, because of thickness, are rarely bound. Instead, seaming ribbon or binding is stitched to them and the edge turned back and slipstitched in place. Bias binding is used on both straight and curved edges, seaming ribbon on straight edges only.

FIG. 1. MACHINE BINDING. When machine binding is used on sheer materials, stay the edge first. Simply turn the edge a scant 1/8 inch and stitch with machine basting. The binding cannot pull off over this stitched edge, a great advantage in garments that are to be washed or materials that fray easily.

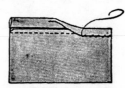

FIG. 3. DOUBLE FOLD BINDING. Binding cut on a true bias twice the width of the binding plus allowance for two narrow seams. Press through the center, stretching slightly in pressing. Stitch binding on. Bring the fold to wrong side and whip down. With very narrow French binding, stitch binding on twice to prevent fraying of narrow seam.

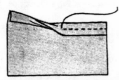

FIG. 2. CENTER STITCHED BINDING. Often in material that has an attractive wrong side, or in which there is no difference in the right and wrong sides, the material itself serves as a binding. Turn the edge to the right side and crease it 1/4 to 3/8 inch. Make a second turn and crease the same depth. Stitch directly through the center of second fold.

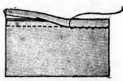

FIG. 4. HAND FELLED BINDING. Stitch the binding on, raw edge brought to wrong side, and whip down. If material frays, first stitch and turn the edge as in Fig. 1, then apply binding.

Machine Hemstitching or Picoting. Chiffon, flimsy georgette, voile, lace, and organdie, and often taffeta and linen, are picoted. This is done in a superior manner at a small cost by most Singer Shops.

Picoting is simply machine hemstitching cut through the center. It makes a beautiful, durable finish, and a desirable one, for delicate fabrics where lightness of effect is essential to style quality.

The beauty of hemstitching or picoting depends largely upon the care used in preparing it for the machine. To prepare material for machine hemstitching, mark with a yard stick or tape and chalk where the hemstitching lines are to come. Then, lest the chalk come off, stitch over these lines with machine basting, using matching thread to avoid the necessity of removing it after hemstitching. If the material is flimsy use paper underneath, as for lace. Remove all paper before sending material to the hemstitcher.

In marking for picoting, space the markings on straight or true bias edges so that when the hemstitching is cut apart both edges of the picoting can be used. For instance, for 3-inch ruffles work the spaces in 6-inch widths; then cut the hemstitching half way between, making 3-inch ruffles.

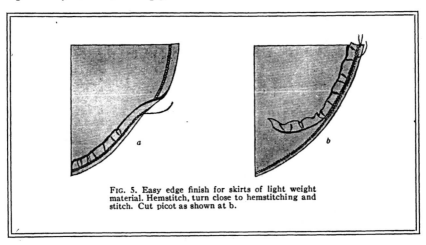

FIG. 5. Easy edge finish for skirts of light weight material. Hemstitch, turn close to hemstitching and stitch. Cut picot as shown at b.

Bound Edges. Binding by machine is the simplest of all ways to finish an edge. It saves times, finishes smartly, gives a desirable weight to the edge, and best of all, it is accomplished in one operation.

Binding may be purchased cut, edges turned, ready for the binder. Number 5 binding works most satisfactorily in the binder. When made at home binding should be cut 15/16 of an inch wide and folded to a width of ½ inch.

When making binding, cut it on a true bias. Join the sections accurately and press them before using. A bias cutting gauge is a real aid in cutting narrow binding or ruffles and may be obtained at small cost at any Singer Shop. Several methods of binding are shown, see Fig. 3. page 4 and page 22. Others will be found in "Short Cuts to Home Sewing", where the Bias Cutting Gauge is shown on page 19.

Neck and Front Finishes

SEVERAL neck finishes are given here that may be used on dresses that have been cut with a regulation neckline. The methods will also serve to finish collar lines according to modern patterns that call for such finishes.

Facings and collars may be made of the material of the dress, or the reverse side of the material, or of contrasting material. The essential is to place next to the face a fabric that in color and texture is becoming to the individual.

Before applying a neck finish to a garment, always be sure that the shoulders are perfectly fitted. Never stretch a neckline in applying a collar, nor crowd any fulness into a narrow collar. Apply a collar with precise regard as to length of neckline so that it fits without effort.

The width of a collar or neck finish should be in harmony with the material used. Firm, heavy materials need usually smaller collars than those of sheer light weight fabrics. Again, a smart style effect may be obtained if an exaggerated or small size collar and cuff effect is employed.

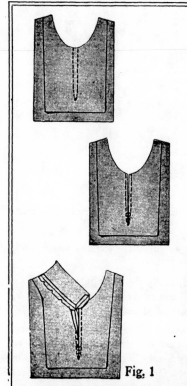

Fig. 1

FIG. 1. REVERE NECK LINE. Three views. The first shows the revere piece applied to the right side of front, the grain and design of the material matching exactly in revere and dress.

To make, stitch on each side of the center front line, which has been marked but not slashed. Stitch down one side and back the other, tapering to a slightly round point at the end of the opening. The length of the opening varies according to styles and types. Slash from the neck down on the center front line to within ⅛ inch of the end of the stitching. The raw edges, because of their narrowness, need special protection at the point. Overcast them two inches up on each side and take several secure overcasting stitches directly at the point so that it cannot fray out. Press the seams open down to the overcasting, turn the revere to the wrong side, and work the seam out to the edge, working around the point carefully so that it will be perfectly smooth and the seam exactly on the edge. Press the revere line downward on the dress so that it will be perfectly flat.

In applying a collar as shown in this group, stitch from the front edge of the revere all the way around to the front edge on the opposite side. Stitch one edge of the collar to the neck and all the way across the back. Stitch the other edge to the revere edges only. Press the seams open that join the collar to the reveres. Clip away the corners of the seams so that they will be smooth. Bring the seams of the collar joining exactly together. Turn in the raw edge of the top collar from shoulder seam to shoulder seam across the back and fell it down covering all seams.

FIG. 2. FACED REVERE. Cut a strip out of the center front of the dress one inch wide, cutting from the neck down the length desired for the revere opening. Cut two pieces for the reveres, cutting them long enough for the opening and wide enough to extend from the center front to two inches beyond the shoulder seams. Stitch these pieces on the right side as shown in the lower figure of group 2. Press the joining seams open and crease on the edges. Bring the revere pieces over and lap them exactly in the center front to fill the cut-out space. Stitch across the bottom, clipping the seam corners first. Smooth the reveres out on the wrong side and whip the overlap at the lower edge on the wrong side. Turn the outside edges in and stitch them free of the dress. Trim the neck edge of the reveres to correspond with the neck edge of the dress and apply the collar the same as in group 1.

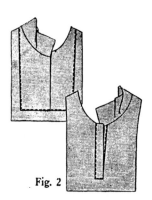

Fig. 2

FIG. 3. OPEN REVERE. Frequently a longer revere line is desired for becomingness than those shown in Fig. 1 and Fig. 2. In such cases apply the revere facings as in Fig. 1, cutting the pieces long enough to extend down as far as desired. Hem the top of the lengthwise vest piece that has been cut wide enough to extend from one edge of the facing piece to the other. Stitch the vest to place as shown, beginning the stitching at the shoulder on each side and stitching down, as far as the vest extends. If it extends only part way down, square it across the front two or three inches below the revere opening. If a larger opening is needed to get into the dress than this gives, lift the vest away on the left side so that it will not be caught in the stitching that extends down from the shoulder. Hem or face the raw edge of the vest and use snap fasteners to hold in place.

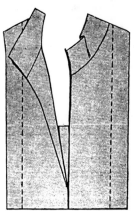

Fig. 3

FIG. 4. RIGHT SIDE REVERE COLLAR APPLIED WITH FLAT BIAS. A revere piece is frequently applied as trimming on the right side, particularly in tailored garments. It may be shaped as shown or as the pattern calls for. In making, place the right side of the revere to the wrong side of the garment, stitch the revere opening, overcast the point, bring the revere to the right side, crease the revere opening neatly on the edge, turn the corners accurately, and stitch them to place. The method of applying the collar as shown in this case is desirable where a loose, easy fitting collar is to result. To make, sew the two collar pieces right sides together, clip the seam, turn right side out. Press, cut true bias about one inch wide, hem on one edge, lay collar on neck line, bias over collar, right side to collar and stitch, clip edges, turn bias in and slipstitch hemmed edge to garment.

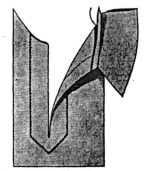

Fig. 4

FIG. 5. SQUARE NECK. To make as shown, cut a true bias strip as wide as desired for the trimming band plus allowance for two seams. Put the dress on and begin at one corner of front neck opening, the half-way point of the band at this corner. Pin at a becoming depth across the front, miter the corners, bring the band over the shoulders and miter the corners accurately. The band should be higher up in the back than in the front. Usually in fitting the band that extends across the back is made longer than that which extends across the front. Smooth the point perfectly on the figure, adjust the corners so that they are true and in harmony with each other, and pin the band securely. When the dress is removed measure the miters one with the other and be sure that they are perfectly straight. Stitch them, keeping the band still pinned to the dress, this to be sure of perfect miters. Remove the band, clip and press the corner seams, place right side of band to wrong side of dress and stitch to position. Notch each corner and turn it to the right side and down. Stitch to place, keeping a true line, and turn corners squarely.

The lower sketch in Fig. 5 shows a square yoke cut without seams. To make a pattern for this, place paper or material on just as you would for a mitered corner square neck. Then place the pattern on the material and cut, omitting the seams. Such a yoke finish is desirable occasionally in using sheer fabric or figured fabrics where seams would be objectionable.

In piping or binding a square neck, if bias is used stretch it at the corners so that it will not wrinkle. If ribbon or braid is used miter neatly at the corners.

Facing neck where fitted facing is not furnished with pattern. Cut bias strips 1¼ inch wide, join and press open seams, turn down one edge and stitch by machine, stretching slightly while stitching—press. Apply raw edge right side to right side of neck, easing in the facing, pin and stitch ¼ inch from edges, turn over baste and slip stitch hem to dress. This mode of facing can be used on other parts of dress, always being careful to ease in on inner curves.

FIG. 6. V NECK. At the left a fitted facing piece is cut with the grain of the dress. This facing piece is stitched to the right side, the point of seam and edges notched. Turn to the right side and add ornamental stitching.

At right is shown a set-in neck. Shape two pieces at the back, seam on the shaped line, and press, the front of dress cut out to desired shape. Turn in the raw edge of cut front and stitch the edges accurately to the set-in piece.

FIG. 7. SLASHED SQUARE NECK. Stitch together the edges of a strip of binding to form buttonhole loops. Cut into 2-inch lengths and catch these in with the binding that finishes the slash. Stitch the binding on and whip down the raw edges, stretching the corners slightly.

FIG. 8. RIBBON BOUND FINISH. Place revere pieces on, wrong side to wrong side of dress, make a slash, join the collar, apply the ribbon, squaring the corners neatly, turn the ends in and stitch to place, one stitching holding both edges.

FIG. 9. DOUBLE BIAS V NECK FINISH. Cut true bias approximately 1½ inches wide. Fold, press. a. Apply raw edge to neck of garment, right side to right side and stitch V in facing. b. Clip V and point. c. Fold bias in middle and stitch on right side in seam with cording foot.

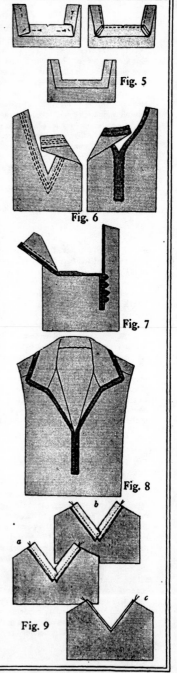

Fig. 5

Fig. 6

Fig. 7

Fig. 8

Fig. 9

Cording

CORDING is done by covering cable cord, or cord made especially for the purpose, with bias pieces of material. The covered cord is inserted in seams used as a finish for an edge, or for shirred bands that give weight or line to garments.

Two things are necessary to perfect cording. They are cable cord of a right size and a cording foot attachment for the sewing machine. Cable cord is soft and limp, a necessary virtue since the weight must blend with a seam. It comes in white and black in several sizes. The smallest size is like carpet warp, the largest is ⅜ inches in diameter.

The cording foot is like a presser foot with the right half cut away. This allows the stitching line to crowd up against the cord and to fit it tightly into place. Yards of cording may be made as easily as a seam, with the attachment, cord, and true bias pieces of material.

In using cording for a dress it is well to cover a generous amount and have it ready so that it may be inserted in a seam or inside a facing when that work is to be done.

Shirred cording is made by applying the material over the cord as for regular cording, then pulling the cord and shirring the material on it by making the cord shorter than the covering. To do this perfectly, use an under piece for the cord covering, stitch it on, draw up the cord, then grasp the edges of the material and pull them in opposite ways to place the shirrings on the cord and make them uniform. This should also be done with puff cordings, where puffings are made in between rows of cording, as in shirred corded trimming bands.

In applying a corded edge to the neck line of a decolleté gown, frequently ends of the cord are left so that they may be drawn up to draw the garment close to the figure. For low neck basque frocks, it is often desirable to draw the edge in to fit more closely. This is easily done when bias cut material covers the cord.

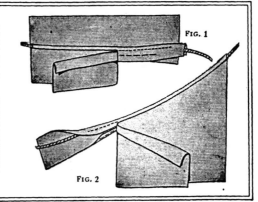

FIG. 1. CORDING A SEAM. Cover the cord, using the cording foot. Pin the seam edges of the covering to one seam of the garment, lap the other seam over this and use the cording foot to join the seam, so the stitching can crowd the seam just as it did when the cord was covered.

FIG. 2. CORDED NECK EDGE. In covering cord for a neck edge, cut the covering, on true bias 1¼ inches wide, turn a ⅜ inch seam over the cord, and stitch the cord in. Stitch the neck edge up against the cord Turn the wide edge of the covering in and stitch it flat as shown. This will conceal the raw edges inside and yet not tighten them, a point necessary on a curved edge.

FIG. 1

FIG. 2

Shirring and Ruffling

THE sewing machine with its ruffler attachment is invaluable in making plaiting and gatherings. No matter what the fashion may be, you need only estimate the correct width and fullness and adjust the ruffler accordingly, to put into your frocks shirrings or gatherings that are in harmony with the mode. To use the ruffler perfectly, read the detailed instructions given on pages 41 to 48 in "Short Cuts to Home Sewing." From these pages you will learn how to adjust the ruffler to accomplish different effects.

Shirrings. The simplest way to shirr is to use the shirring foot. By loosening the tension and lengthening stitch, you may guide by the edge of foot or mark each row. In making fine shirrings, use fine thread and place the rows closer together than for material that is coarser or heavier.

In making group shirrings at the top of a sleeve or in a yoke, cut a piece of net the shape of the plain sleeve or dress yoke and sew this as lining under the shirring. This will prevent unnecessary strain on the shirred portion and protect the shirrings at the same time.

The more sheer the fabric, the more fulness is required to get the right effect. With chiffon, frequently twice the width is used in making shirrings. For plain shirrings in voile or georgette, usually one and one-half times the width desired for the completed shirred portion is sufficient allowance. For example, if a piece of shirring a yard wide is required, the piece before it is shirred should measure 1½ yards.

When shirrings are done in a yoke or sleeves, a plain pattern is placed over the shirred portions and the garment shaped as desired. If a pattern is used that provides for shirring, then use a longer stitch in making the shirrings than for regular sewing, so that the shirring threads can be drawn up or let out to fit the foundation or stay pieces.

In making many rows of shirring, use the tucker, with needle unthreaded, to mark the spaces evenly, or stitch rows of tucks, using a long stitch and drawing the threads up to make shirrings of the tucks.

Shirrings have two virtues in that they decorate and soften the lines of a garment. Soft limp materials of fine weave such as voile, chiffon, georgette, flat crepe and velvet are preferred where shirrings are to be used. Machine stitching should appear fine. The length of the stitch therefore should be such as to appear fine when the stitching is drawn to place.

Ruffling. In applying ruffles in tiers on a skirt, the ruffles should overlap from one to two inches. The best plan is to measure the width of the ruffles and to measure the skirt, and crease on the lines where the ruffles are to come. Place the ruffles on, hem side turned up on the dress, and sew them on so that when they are dropped back to position, the raw edges will be concealed.

Collars and Cuffs

SIMPLE frocks gain new charm when finished with smart collars and cuffs. One and two piece dresses can be made quite plain, and with becoming collar and cuffs obtain a distinctive effect.

Collars and cuffs used on simple frocks as a distinctive trimming feature are made most frequently of organdie, georgette, batiste, pique, linen or ribbon, the color and size depending always upon their becomingness and the dictates of fashion. A tiny collar band an inch wide may be used, or a bertha may extend all the way to the waist line. The Dutch, Buster Brown, or Robespierre collars appear from time to time as a feature of fashion and may usually be adapted to individual taste. The shape, color, texture and trimming should be considered, because collars and cuffs must be perfectly designed and made to seem to belong entirely to a frock and complement it, rather than appear as extra pieces.

In using patterns to cut collars and cuffs, always consider well the fabric and the effect to be produced. Frequently it is advisable to cut the pattern pieces down, or make them a little larger, that the proportions of the collar and cuffs be right for the individual and for the frock on which they are worn.

Again, when a fashion effect is designed and a pattern cannot be obtained that is exactly right, it is a good idea to take an inexpensive fabric that is of a texture similar to that which you are going to use, and pin the collar and cuffs to the figure and shape them as you want them. In doing this it is always advisable to place the fold of the material at the center back and work around toward the front. In making the collar, fold the pattern, pinning it or slashing it to make it flare or shape to place in keeping with the design being copied.

The sewing machine is the perfect medium for making smart collars and cuffs. Tiny tucks made with the tucker in crossbar or diagonal shapes, or all-over tucking with edges bound or lace trimmed or faced, are always in some form favored by fashion, and the woman who knows the beauty of dainty tucking, seaming, binding and stitching will be able to achieve smart effects with little money and effort. Always bind the inside edges of collars and cuffs with narrow binding to serve as a foundation in basting them on the garment.

In planning collars and cuffs, remember that the best effect is obtained when they contrast in texture with the material of the dress, although it is not necessary that they contrast in color.

Leather or suede collars and cuffs are often very appropriate and add a note of chic to sports frocks. Metallic or fur collars and cuffs are at times equally smart on frocks of silk crepe or satin. Usually a larger needle and coarser thread are necessary in stitching such materials.

29

Tailoring the Modern Way

THE modern definition of tailoring is perfect seaming and stitching, especially where the stitching shows. To know how to stitch, blend and press a seam is to know the essentials of tailoring.

Modern tailoring is applied to sheerest frocks and daintiest lingerie. In fact, in modern sewing all things are considered tailored that are not lace or ribbon trimmed.

The shoulders shown here, for instance, must be perfectly tailored to shape correctly and to give distinction to the garment of which they are a part. Each part must be fitted into place accurately, the seams clipped and pressed in the right direction to allow the bulk or weight of the garment to set into its proper place. In the epaulet shoulder, for instance, where a shirred seam joins a plain one, the shirred seam is always turned back on the plain one to give balance. Notice carefully how the seam corners are cut at the shoulder points in Fig. 1. The seam is slashed and turned in toward the shoulder piece. In the case of the sleeves, the seam is slashed and the seam turned in toward the dress. This makes it necessary to cut the shoulder seam all the way into the stitching line and to overcast the corners securely so that it will not fray.

In a raglan shoulder, Fig. 2, it is necessary after a perfect seam has been made to notch the seam every two inches as shown to allow the seam to shape itself properly to the shoulder. After making seams such as the two shown here, stitch the sleeve and under-arm seams in one operation.

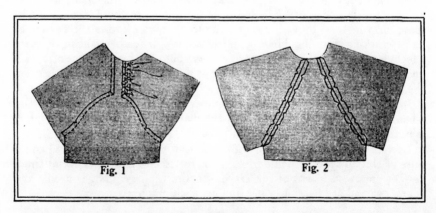

Fig. 1   Fig. 2

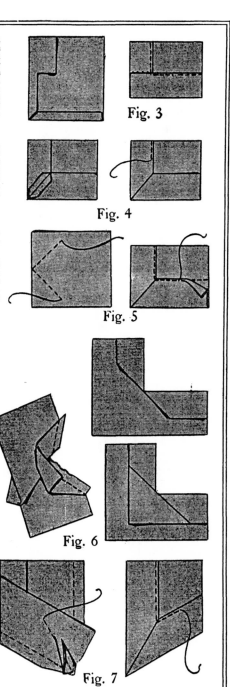

Fig. 3. A Straight Corner. At the left you see exactly how to trim the surplus thickness away inside the corner so that when the hem is brought up the corner will be flat. The left end of the hem, as well as that which overlaps the first hem, should be whipped to place. Turn the corner accurately in the machine stitching and continue on from corner to corner, catching the hem all the way.

Fig. 3

Fig. 4. A Bias Corner. At the left you see just how the edges are brought together on the wrong side for a true bias miter, how the seams join, and how the seam is clipped slantwise at both ends to allow it to fit into place when the hem is turned right side out, as shown at the right.

Fig. 4

Fig. 5. Applied Mitered Band. Often on an unlined coat or on panel edges, or as a trimming feature for a dress, a double band is added to an edge. Determine the width of the band to be used when the dress is cut. Cut all the bands on the length twice the width of the finished band plus the seams' allowance. To gain true corner, fold lengthwise strip, creasing center. Bring crosswise fold to center crease. Stitch on bias crease as shown. At the right you see the manner of application.

Fig. 5

Fig. 6. A Stayed Corner. To finish off a square cut section so that the corner will not fray when the seams are turned back, as shown in the upper right figure of Fig. 6, cut a small square of light-weight material, silk for wool, silk for silk and light-weight cotton for linen. Then cut the square diagonally across. Sew the bias edge to the corner, as shown at the left, taking a very narrow seam, especially at the point of the corner. Turn the applied corner over to the wrong side, press, and shape it in place so that it will appear as shown at the lower right of Fig. 6.

Fig. 6

Fig. 7. Pointed Trimming Band. Applying a lengthwise band to a pointed collar or cuff is done by stitching the band to the wrong side of the collar or cuff the full length of the outside edge. Stitch exactly to a point and clip off the end of the seam. Miter the point in a long seam as shown at the left. Press the seam open, turn the band to the right side, and stitch it flat as shown.

Fig. 7

Applied Trimmings and Finishes

IT is a time honored fashion to use the material of the dress itself for trimming. Occasionally variation is made through the use of contrasting color, or by using the reverse side of the fabric. Fashion also favors at times fabrics with design trimmed with plain material, or plain fabrics trimmed with design material.

The discriminating dressmaker uses materials, widths and sizes in trimmings that are chic and flattering and that add value and distinction to the garment she makes. Trimmings should belong so perfectly to a garment it would seem incomplete without them. Then and then only are they successful.

Current fashions should guide one to a smart use of fabric trimming. The methods given here are versatile enough to guide one in developing similar trimming effects and to have them in accord with fashion.

Fig. 1

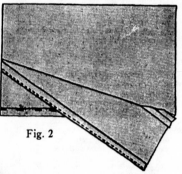

Fig. 2

Sew the buttons securely but loosely so that they will not crowd the band tight against the garment.

To make bands to fagot to a garment, proceed in the same way. Baste the edge of the garment and the band on firm strips of paper, spacing them apart according to the width desired for the fagotting stitches. When the stitches are in, press the band and edge thoroughly, then remove the paper.

FIG. 1. APPLIED BUTTONHOLE BAND. Width of the band may vary from ¼ inch to 3 inches. It may be made of material of the dress or contrasting. It may be plain or have ornamented stitching applied.

To make, stitch and turn as for a belt. Finish the edge that is to join. Press the band and garment edges and pin the band to place, spacing the pins accurately and a distance apart to provide even spaces for the buttons to slip through. Replace the pins with secure stitches of buttonhole twist, made loose enough to allow the band to press down flat.

FIG. 2. FACING. When a facing is used to finish an edge, pin the facing to the edge and stitch it to place. Keep the facing side up as you stitch. Clip the seam every 3 or 4 inches and press it open. If the facing is of the material of the dress, press directly on the edge. If lighter weight material is used, the seam should come in a seam's width from the edge on the facing side. Seam pressed open as shown. Baste along the seam and press the facing, pressing from the edge in. Secure the free edge of the facing to the garment with slip stitches or ornamental stitching done on the right side.

Making Pockets

ONCE the principle is understood, pocket making is easy. There are bound, patch, welt and stand pockets. Some one of these is invariably in fashion's favor, and frequently all are considered smart.

The size of the pocket is an important fashion point and one the pattern usually takes care of. If, however, you shorten or lengthen the garment, take care to mark the new pocket location, and if necessary, alter the size of the pocket itself. When two pockets are used, one on each side of a garment, fold the garment together with the center front line exactly on the fold, and mark each side the same. When trying for slenderness, avoid having pockets too far apart or too broad. Short figures should avoid large pockets; large figures, small ones.

Fashion places pockets in many ways. Inserted pockets may be straight across, vertical or diagonal in a garment. The difference is in the shaping of the pocket pouch. The method of making will always be the same.

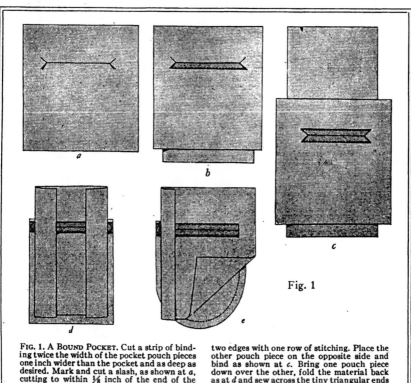

Fig. 1

FIG. 1. A BOUND POCKET. Cut a strip of binding twice the width of the pocket pouch pieces one inch wider than the pocket and as deep as desired. Mark and cut a slash, as shown at *a*, cutting to within ⅛ inch of the end of the line. Then cut in a forked line at each end, cutting the forks only ¼ inch deep. Pin one pouch piece to one edge of the slashed seam and bind together, as at *b*, placing the binding on in a perfectly straight line and joining the two edges with one row of stitching. Place the other pouch piece on the opposite side and bind as shown at *c*. Bring one pouch piece down over the other, fold the material back as at *d* and sew across the tiny triangular ends of the slash. Stitch these ends twice across as in *e*, so that they cannot pull out. Finally trim the lower edge of the pouch, rounding the corners neatly. Stitch as shown at *e*, and complete the pocket by pressing.

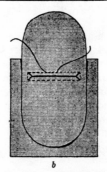

a   b   c

FIG. 2. A WELT STAND POCKET. Cut, as at *a*, an oblong piece of material the same in grain and design as the garment. Place the right side of the material to the right side of the garment. Baste it to place as the center line shows. Stitch all the way around, making an oblong box. Begin the stitching at the center of one line rather than at a corner. Cut on the basting line, as shown at *b*, to within ⅜ inch of the ends; then cut diagonally to the corners. Pull the pouch pieces through to the wrong side, and pull the lower one up to fill the slash or box, thus forming a stand or weit. Hold this welt to place by stitching it through the seam of the slash as at *c*, but not through the garment. Bring the upper piece down over the welt piece and stitch all around the pouch as in Fig. 1. Sew ends of the welt to this, first from wrong side, then from right.

To make a welt pocket in a wool garment, use silk for the pouch with a lengthwise strip of the wool material for the welt. Cut this welt one inch longer than the pocket and two inches wide. Baste the right side of the strip, or welt piece, to the right side of the garment. Place the pouch piece over this and stitch and slash the same as at *a* and *b*. Turn the pouch piece to the wrong side, bring the applied welt piece from each side of the slash to fill it up. The welt effect appears the same as for the bound pocket, except that no stitching shows on the right side. Stitch the pouch, secure the ends on both sides, and press.

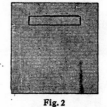

Fig. 2

d

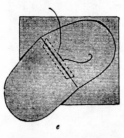

e   f   g

FIG. 3. A STAND POCKET. To make a stand pocket, first stitch the ends of the stand as shown at *d*. Clip the corners and turn it right side out. Place the stand next to the right side of the garment, the folded edge of the stand down. Place the pouch piece on as shown at *e*. Place a stay piece cut lengthwise directly underneath as at *f*. Stitch as shown in these two details, beginning at the center of one side. Slant the stitch slightly at the ends, as shown both in *e* and *f*. Cut a slash between the pocket pouches and the forked ends, but do not cut beyond the stitching. Pull the pocket pieces through and work the ends out neatly. Stitch around the pouch as at *g*, overcast the raw edges, and catch-stitch the ends of pouch and stay pieces as shown.

Fig. 3

With right sides of material together, sew pocket piece to garment as illustrated.

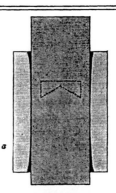

a

Cut out material about ⅝ inch inside of stitching, cutting corners to stitching. Pull pocket through to wrong side, creasing in seams.

a

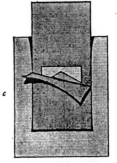

Fold pocket material ¼ inch from lower corner toward top of pocket. Fold same piece back the other way on line even with upper edge of pocket, forming stand.

b

b

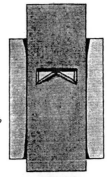

c

c

Stitch on right side ends and point. Bring upper piece down under stand piece to form pocket and stitch across opening to meet other stitching. ¼ inch from end of upper stitching, stitch two pieces together completing pocket. Pink raw edges.

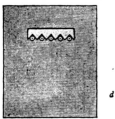

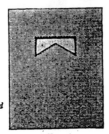

d

d

FIG. 5   FIG. 6

Bound Buttonholes

BUTTONHOLES on smart frocks are most often bound either of fabric or with ribbon braid or binding. Fashion determines the size and shape of buttons and they in turn indicate the size for buttonholes. Once the method is understood, they may be made in any way required.

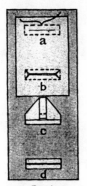

FIG. 1

FIG. 2

FIG. 3

FIG. 1. FABRIC BOUND BUTTONHOLES. First cut a lengthwise strip of material 1 inch wider than the buttonholes and long enough to extend the full length of the buttonhole edge. For example, if there are to be 8 buttonholes 2 inches apart and 1 inch wide, take a strip approximately 2 inches wide and 18 inches long. Place it on the right side of the garment as in Fig. 1. Mark with a ruler and chalk just where the buttonholes are to come. Stitch an oblong slot as at a around the marking, making the slot exactly as you do a pocket slash, cutting out to within ¼ inch of the end, then forking the end to the corners of the stitching, as at b. Overcast the slash. Slash the buttonhole strip half way between the buttonholes, pull the welt through to the wrong side, as at c. Pull the welt up even, to fill the slot, so that the finished buttonhole will appear as at d. Overcast the welt edges together, simply to hold the edges securely while the raw edges on the wrong side are whipped to place, and until pressed.

FIG. 2. CORDED BUTTONHOLE. Cut true bias strip approximately 1¼ inches wide, fold with cord in center. Mark place for buttonhole. With cording foot stitch bias enclosing cord to right side of material allowing ¼ inch on each end not stitched to garment. This should be placed about ⅛ inch from mark indicating place for buttonhole. Stitch similar piece ⅛ inch from first piece between corded pieces in forked line as Fig. 2, page 36, pull through to wrong side. Fold material back and stitch across tiny triangular ends of slash and bias. On right side stitch in seam between garment and cording.

FIG. 3. FOLDED FABRIC BUTTONHOLE. Cut strip 1 inch wider than buttonhole and long enough to cover row of buttonholes. Turn edges of strip ¼ inch. Baste strip in place, right side to right side of garment, with machine basting along line of buttonhole. Stitch ⅛ inch being careful not to stitch beyond. Cut through both thicknesses of material along basted line, but not through edge of applied piece. Cut applied piece in middle between buttonholes. Pull through to wrong side, folding pieces so that the crease meets in middle of buttonhole, press, trim off extra material, turn under and stitch once, blind stitch.

FIG. 4. TUBE LOOPS. When many loops are used for buttonholes and where no machine stitching shows. Place a piece of small cord inside a bias strip making a narrow seam. Catch one end of the cord by stitches over the end as shown. Pull the cord and push the tube off, which will turn the seam inside out of the stitched end, and pull the cord away. Press this tubing and use it for loops, placing them inside a seam or edge as in Fig. 4.

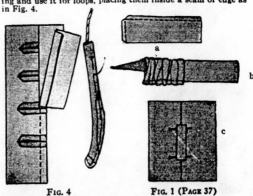

FIG. 4   FIG. 1 (PAGE 37)

Belts and Ties

IN making narrow belts always cut them on the true lengthwise grain twice the width desired for the finished belt, plus ¼ inch seams. Cut as long as desired; if piecing is necessary, arrange the piecings to come at the side seams of the dress. Seam the edges as at *a*, Fig. 1. Place the seam at the edge for light weight or sheer materials. For heavier fabrics, press the seam open and arrange to have it come at the center of one side. Always press the seam open no matter where its position. Sew across one end. Place the stub end of a pencil against the seam at the end of the belt and proceed to push the belt through as at *b*, continuing until the belt is turned right side out. Press the belt again.

When a single belt is used, make belt straps of tiny strips of the material. Turn the seam right side out and pin the belt to place, usually with the seam directly over the side seams at a becoming waist line position. Sew the end of the straps securely so that the stitches do not show.

In making sash ties that tie in a bow, cut them on a true bias or on a slant bias with the lower edges wider than the top.

FIG. 2. TWO BELTS. Often two narrow belts are used, one placed a little above the other. Tailored bows of the belt strip are cut and sewed flat to cover the belt joining.

FIG. 3. STITCHED-IN BELT. The waist part shaped as shown, two tabs cut in front and back, the seams turned back accurately, inside corners clipped. Belts inserted underneath the tabs and spaced ⅛ inch apart, the tabs stitched down to hold the belt sections to place. A slide buckle may be used or not in the lower strap.

FIG. 4. A POCKET BELT. Put the top hem in and turn the edges of the tiny patch pockets. Place two narrow belts at the waist line and stitch the pockets directly over these. Buttons may be used on the pockets or crosswise at the waist line in a space between the pockets.

FIG. 5. AN INSERTED BELT. Cut two belts, place the under one so that the seams will come to the right side. Cover the seams neatly with the remaining piece. Stitch at the edges, keeping a straight line.

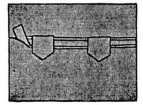

Fig. 2

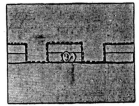

Fig. 3

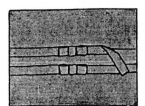

Fig. 4

Fig. 5

Plaiting

THERE are many forms of plaiting. Each season it comes to us in varied forms.

Accordion plaits must be steam plaited so that they will hold in place. Others, such as inverted, box or knife plaits having a width of one inch or more can easily be made at home. Narrow plaiting for trimming can be made with the Singer Ruffler.

To prepare material for steam plaiting, tear the fabric or pull a thread, making the lengths as desired plus the hem and waist line finish. Prepare three times as much width as you require for finished use. Stitch widths together, leaving one seam open. Make flat, pressed open seams and flat hems. If the material is heavy, face the lower edge with lighter weight material, or picot it so there is no bulk. Send the material for plaiting to the shop specializing in this work.

Place the plaited material in position in the garment before sewing the open seam so that any necessary adjustment can be made.

When making inverted, box or knife plaits in skirts, determine the length, stitch all seams in the skirt, turn the hem and arrange the plaits. Crease plaits on the lengthwise thread. If piecings must be made, arrange them so that the seams come in the inside of the plaits. Join the piecings with a plain, unopened seam, clip it and press it open inside the hem. Machine bastings are ideal in holding plaits in making and pressing and make them easy to iron. In pressing use a damp cloth and press from the right side. See page 45 of "Short Cuts to Home Sewing" for making plaiting with the machine Ruffler.

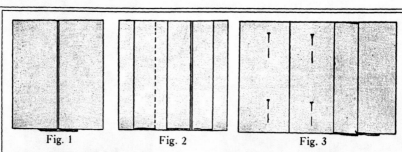

Fig. 1   Fig. 2   Fig. 3

FIG. 1. INVERTED PLAITS. Turn the edges together, making plait the same distance no each side. Pin and machine baste underneath the edges. Hold the two top edges together with long, diagonal basting.

FIG. 2. BOX PLAITS. Measure and space the plaits, pinning each one. Stitch with machine basting as shown. Press the plaits flat, the seam in the center on the under side. Remove the basting from the bottom up, leaving enough basting at the top to hold the plaits to place.

FIG. 3. KNIFE PLAITS. Crease the lengthwise edges of the plaits, using pins to mark the placings. Fold the plaits over and press. Allow ¼ inch space between each plait so that they will not overlap.

Tucking

IN TUCKING parts of a dress it is best to take two widths of material wide enough and long enough to allow for the amount the tucks will take up. Place the tucking to conform to the style effect desired. Press the tucking after it is made and then cut the material as though it were plain fabric, using a plain, foundation pattern. When placing the pattern on take care that the tucks come to correct position for the desired style effect.

Tucks may be minute in width or as wide as plaits. The tiniest tucks are called pin tucks and made only a pin's width from the creased edge. Tucks should be made on the true lengthwise, crosswise or bias grains, to insure that they press evenly and do not twist.

Tucks that come inside a garment and not at a seam edge should have the stitches pulled back with a pin so that all rows are perfectly even. Pull the threads through to the wrong side at the ends of each row and tie them securely. In using very sheer materials, such as organdie, when starting the tuck, run back on the first few stitches to fasten the stitch. The same is done at the other end of the tuck. Ends can then be cut close without tying and will not show through.

Materials best for tucking are those that have a slight "body."

The machine tucker with its infallible marker is a wonderful aid in doing exact work and tucking must be perfect since it is a decorative feature. Instructions are given for the tucker, also its adjustment to different widths, on pages 36 to 40 of "Short Cuts to Home Sewing."

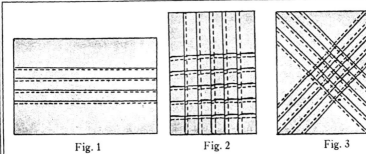

Fig. 1   Fig. 2   Fig. 3

FIG. 1. STRAIGHT TUCKING. Tucks an even width and distance apart. Used to give weight or as trimming for an edge, usually both. Tucks may be wide or narrow, spacing and width depending on the effect desired.

FIG. 2. CROSS TUCKING. Tucks are placed one way, as in Fig. 1, pressed, and cross tucking applied directly over these. Skill in holding the fabric is essential so that the squares will be true and the tucks will not slip out of line in stitching.

FIG. 3. BIAS TUCKING. Follow the marker exactly. Hold the fabric firm but do not stretch it. Use paper under the marker so that the creases will be definite enough to follow easily.

Making a Two Piece Dress

THE two-piece dress comes and goes as the fashions change with the passing of the seasons and its popularity and smartness change accordingly. Despite style or season there are certain detail facts usually true of almost any two-piece dress. The skirt usually has fullness provided either by circular flare, godets or plaits, and is held up by a bodice. Such a dress requires one-half yard more material than a one-piece, as well as enough material for the bodice lining.

In selecting a pattern for a two-piece dress with an under bodice, choose one that has darts either at the under-arm or the front shoulder of the bodice to allow ease across the bust and to lift the under-arm seam.

The foundation bodice with skirt usually slips over the head, no opening or plaquet is made. Put the darts in the under-arm as in Fig. 1, page 41, join the shoulder and under-arm seams and put narrow binding or facing at the neck and armhole. In finishing the neck line, take care to have it low enough so that it will not show above the neck line of the dress. When binding or facing the armholes, cut away a generous seam's width before applying, so that the armhole will not be tight. Finally stitch the lower edge of the bodice to the skirt.

In making a two-piece dress with plaited skirt, no pattern is really needed for the skirt. Simply cut the skirt length long enough to allow for hem and waist line seam. Sew enough widths together to give the desired fullness in the skirt, two 40-inch widths usually providing ample. Put the hem in the bottom according to amount allowed.

Arrange the plaits to absorb the fullness, bringing the top of the skirt in to a measurement that is in accord with the measurement at the top of the hips, or where the skirt is to join the bodice lining.

In making the dress, if the pattern calls for tucks across the back neck, or if the garment would fit better by the addition of tucks, stitch them in as in Fig. 3, page 41, beginning the stitching at the neck and tapering down two inches. If sheer material is being used, tucks should be stitched with single thread as explained in Fig. 1. b, page 17. If shirrings in the front shoulder are planned for, use machine basting and space them from ⅛ to ⅜ inches apart. The spacings depend upon the number of rows used and the effect desired. Draw the threads up as in Fig. 4, page 41, so that when the fullness is adjusted the front shoulder will allow the back shoulder to be eased to it. When the shirrings have been drawn to place, tie the machine threads or stitch over them at the ends. The Singer gathering foot may also be used to do this shirring in one operation.

A two-piece dress is a blouse and skirt made to assemble as a dress. If the blouse is short, the skirt should be cut long enough or a band of the skirt material should be used at the bottom of the bodice, so that in stooping, the bodice material will not show.

When the sleeves are stitched to place in the armhole, overcast the armhole seams, or stitch them twice by machine, the second row ¼ inch out on the seam.

A two-piece dress may be made to do double duty and play the game of transformations to a winning finish if one is clever in choosing and combining fabrics to suit the occasions. Several blouses for business or for afternoon tea may be worn successfully with the one well chosen bodice and skirt as the need arises.

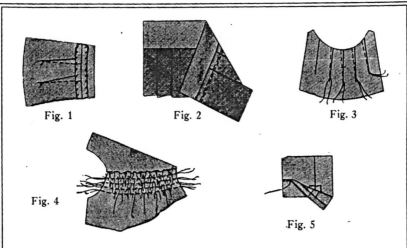

Fig. 1   Fig. 2   Fig. 3

Fig. 4

Fig. 5

FIG. 1. UNDER-ARM DARTS. Under-arm sag drawn up to give straight waist line and ease over bust. Amount taken up divided in two darts which taper to a point two to three inches from seam.

FIG. 2. WAIST LINE JOINING. Machine baste across plaits to hold them. Join bodice to skirt, under-arm seams meeting. Stitch in plain seam below row of basting.

FIG. 3. BACK NECK TUCKS. ¼-inch tucks two inches deep and tapered to a point with thread ends tied. Serves to control fulness and

shorten shoulder widths. When sheer materials are used, tucks may be stitched with single thread the same as darts shown in Fig. 1, b, page 17.

FIG. 4. SHIRRED SHOULDERS. Place rows of machine bastings even distances apart and draw up even for shirrings. Fasten thread ends. Pin and stitch to back shoulders.

FIG. 5. RIGHT SIDE HEM. Stitch seam to wrong side to a point twice width of hem desired. Slash seam across; turn seam to right side; stitch; press open; lap hem over seam.

Making a Party Dress

THE bodice dress appears each season in varied form. It is ideal for graduation or as a party frock for girls or slender women. For variation the bodice may be longer or shorter. The sleeves may have a drop shoulder, or be set in, or there may be no sleeves. The neck line may be V, or square, or both. The skirt longer or shorter, or have an uneven hem line. It may be cut for shirrings at the waist line, or be circular. Usually it is shirred because of the fullness. The waist line is often corded and sometimes stitched plain. The lower edge may be bound, or have ruffles, or bands of the material itself, or of contrasting material or a double fold of net attached to a bound scalloped lower edge.

To make a simple bodice dress, first put the shirrings, tucks, or darts in the shoulders, Fig. 1, pulling the thread ends through to the wrong side and tying them. Join the shoulder seams. Bind the neck and armhole edges; or a fitted corded facing may be used. Stitch the right under-arm seam in the blouse, and the left one down to within six inches of the waist line. Stitch the right seam of the skirt, and stitch the left seam to within four inches of the waist line. Shirr the top of the skirt and join it to the bodice, taking care that the fullness of the shirrings is evenly distributed. To make the plaquet, finish the under-arm opening as in Fig. 2. To do this, cut straight strips making them a little longer than the opening and one and one-half inches wide. Sew the right side of the strips to the wrong side of the dress, bring the free edges over, stitch the under one flat, and sew long eyes on the edge. The hooks, except the prongs, are covered by the straight piece.

For a simple skirt, put the hem in, as in Fig. 1, page 21, hem the narrow ruffles, put a row of shirring in the center as in Fig. 3, and apply as shown.

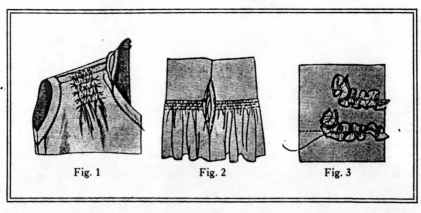

Fig. 1   Fig. 2   Fig. 3

Making a Sleeveless Dress

THE sleeveless dress is frequently made so that sleeves may be adjusted in the armholes when desired, and be worn without sleeves when a sleeveless dress is in order. It represents a foundation type of dress, one that can be varied in many ways to get different effects. The materials used are as varied as the uses of the sleeveless dress, governed only by the dictates of the season. When making the dress of lace or chiffon cut it slightly larger than for satin or velvet, because the heavier materials can becomingly fit more snugly.

The neck may be square, V or round, in accordance with the fashion of the moment and becomingness to the individual.

If the fabric is sheer, the dart fullness under the arm is usually gathered, Fig 2. If the fabric is firm, place darts as shown on page 41, Fig. 1. Follow pattern construction chart step by step as procedure varies a little from time to time according to the pattern being used.

For a circular skirt, piece the lower part if necessary as in Fig. 1, pressing the seams as shown. After side seams are stitched, hang it up to sag, if possible for a day, before finishing the bottom.

If a belt is used, determine its place, pinning it carefully. Then adjust the skirt and even the hem line preparatory to finishing.

When binding finishes the bottom of the skirt, have the skirt one inch longer than for a hem because the binding will tend to shorten the dress somewhat; also, a dress that has no hem will shorten in pressing. Fig. 6, page 23 gives a very good hem finish for sheer materials. Before hemstitching, a thread should be run to indicate the position of the hemstitching, as shown in Fig. 3.

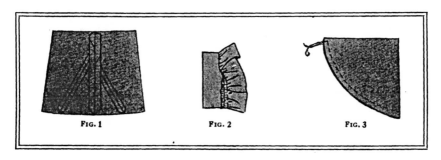

FIG. 1   FIG. 2   FIG. 3

Making a Coat

COATS like all other articles of apparel vary according to season and vogue. But there are certain fundamental principles that always apply.

If wool material is used, shrink it first. A simple way to do this is to take an old sheet or length of muslin, wet it in warm water, and wring it as dry as possible. Lay it out on the table, place the material over it, and roll in an even, smooth improvised roll of newspaper as a base. Let it remain for six to ten hours, and then remove it and hang it over a line or door to dry. Cotton and linen fabrics can be shrunk in the same manner. Shrunken fabrics will not need pressing before cutting if the roll is carefully done and no wrinkles allowed to form.

Buy the same size pattern as for a dress. If the coat is unlined, cut the seams deeper than the pattern calls for. The coat pattern itself is used to cut the lining. To do this place the back of the coat pattern one inch in from the fold, this to make a plait to provide necessary ease in putting the coat on and off. Turn the front of the pattern back at the line that indicates the edge of front facing, usually marked with medium perforations on the pattern. The lining meets the facing edge and does not extend all the way to the front.

Make a knife plait of the allowance in the back of the lining, basting and pressing it to place. Stitch up the under-arm seams and press them open. Leave the shoulder seams open. Stitch the sleeve seams, clip and press them, thus making the lining ready to join to the coat.

Cut an inside facing piece of light weight muslin. Use the front of the pattern for this and cut it the same as the facing, less the seam allowance at the center front. Place the inside facing to the coat and baste it to position as in Fig. 1, page 45. Stitch and press the front facing seams, crease and baste on the edge.

Put the darts in the front of the coat and join the shoulder, underarm and sleeve seams, clip these seams and press them open. Turn and finish the edges of the pockets as in Fig. 2, page 45, and pin the pockets to place on the coat.

When fitting the coat, lap it correctly in the front and pin from the bottom up. If the coat seems wide in the shoulder line, put tiny tucks in the back as shown in Fig. 3, page 41. Determine in fitting the perfection of fit in the shoulders and make any advisable adjustments. Mark the length for the sleeves and for the coat at the bottom, and verify the position of the pockets.

Place the interlining in the collar, seam the outside edges, blend and press the seams, clip the corners, and turn the collar right side out. Stitch the body and shoulder seams of the coat and press them thoroughly. Join the collar to the coat, stitching it on the same as for a revere collar, Fig. 1, page 24. Put in the bound buttonholes, turn the edge of the facing in and whip it down to the under side of the buttonholes so that they will appear as neat on the wrong side as on the right. Join the cuff seams and press them open, using interlining if the material is light weight.

Put in the ornamental stitching, if any, continuously in the collar and front edges, squaring the corners perfectly, also stitch the cuffs and pockets.

Stitch and press open the sleeve seams of the coat, and apply the cuffs as in Fig. 3, page 46. After the cuffs are joined, place the lining of the sleeve in, pinning the sleeve seams of the coat to the seams in the lining. Baste the seam edges together, taking the basting stitches so that they may remain in. Turn the lower edge of the sleeve lining under and whip it down, covering all raw edges. Pin and baste the sleeve in the armholes and slip the coat on to verify shoulder seams and sleeve position. Stitch the sleeves in, catching the lining in with the sleeves.

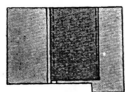

FIG. 1

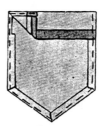

FIG. 2

FIG. 1. INSIDE FACING. Light weight shrunken muslin caught to the pressed open seam edge with long basting stitches; caught also the coat; all stitches taken so that they do not show on the right side. Lower edge of facing cut to make plain seam across the bottom.

FIG. 2. TAILORED PATCH POCKETS. Seaming ribbon is placed over hem edge of the pocket. Seams inside the hem trimmed away to avoid bulk. Seams at the points also notched to make a flat seam at these points.

Catstitch the hem in the bottom of the coat as in Fig. 4. Go over the coat quite thoroughly to make sure that every part has been perfectly finished. Sponge and press the coat in its entirety, making it ready for the lining.

Put the coat over a dress form, wrong side out and pin the lining to place, beginning at the center back. Stitch the front edges of the lining to the back edge of the front facing and press the seams open. To do this stitching it is necessary to turn the coat inside out. Baste the side seams of the lining to the side seams of the coat. Lap the shoulder seams of the lining and pin in a true, even line. Turn and pin the raw edges in around the collar line and the armholes. Whip these pinned edges to place, using close, secure whipping stitches. Put the coat on, mark the position of the buttons and sew them on. Remove all threads, and press the coat thoroughly, when it is ready for wear.

FIG. 3. APPLIED CUFFS. Inside edge of cuff stitched to bottom of sleeve in half-inch seam, seams in cuff and sleeve meeting. Seams trimmed to ¼ inch width. Ends of seams clipped diagonally. Right side of cuff brought to wrong side of sleeve and catstitched to place in readiness for lining.

FIG. 3

FIG. 4

FIG. 5

FIG. 4. FRONT FACING. Shows how the jog line in Fig. 1 is brought to place, seam made at lower edge of front facing, and hem catstitched to coat and edge of facing.

FIG. 5. LINING JOINED TO FACING. Seam where lining joins facing, pressed open. Lining edge turned up half the width of coat hem and stitched to place.

FIG. 6

FIG. 7

FIG. 6. LINING AND HEM JOINED. Where material of lining or coat ravels easily, hem of coat should be slipstitched to place, edge of lining and hem stitched together. Stitches show lower part of lining holding tuck in back of lining to place at lower edge of coat.

FIG. 7. CORD COVERED LOOPS. Used for light-weight fabrics as fasteners where buttonholes are not desirable. Cord is covered, ends turned under and sewed securely but inconspicuously to edge of coat. Upper loop shows wrong side, lower loop right side.

Style and Construction

WHEN perfection has been attained in joining shoulder, under-arm and sleeve seams, the joining, stitching and pressing all done with skill and satisfaction, when your knowledge and deftness in using your machine has made it your perfect servant, then the art of dressmaking will tempt you to new adventures in the creation of smart clothes.

The essential quality—style—is a tangible, attainable asset which every dress must possess to have distinctive value. Three yards of flat crepe costing two dollars a yard can be made into an ordinary ten dollar dress, or with the magic touch of style, the same material can be converted into a thirty dollar frock. A dress of satin costing four dollars per yard, through its style or lack of it represents a fifty or a fifteen dollar value. Your responsibility is to make your dress as valuable as possible from a style point of view. To do this, determine from a study of current fashions what in the mode will be most becoming and smartest for you, and then set out to create for yourself a dress that is in every way perfect.

Go over the clothes you have. Rip up a dress of good material but obsolete in style and re-cut and re-make it. Occasionally combining other materials with what you have is an economy and an advantage from a style point of view. Put on a dress of last season, see how it differs from the current mode and what styling will be necessary in re-making it to be in keeping with the mode. Modern sewing is accomplished so easily that to re-make a dress is no problem. The problem is to style a dress so that it takes on value in your hands. Garments of good material, no matter how old, can be ripped, washed, re-dyed if necessary, and entirely rejuvenated. Garments of good material have value as long as style quality is retained in them.

When you have mastered the art of garment construction, when you understand the foundation seams and how to stitch them, when you are thoroughly familiar with all the finishes and know how to make them not only perfectly but smartly, resolve that you will never make ordinary dresses, but always interesting ones. Approach the making of a dress as an artist would approach a picture, keeping in mind from the very start the effect you want in the finished frock. Visualize the dress complete before you even buy the material. If you have an illustration from a fashion magazine or a pattern to guide you, look at this several times during the making of your dress, so that you retain the original idea and that your dress when finished will have in it not only perfect construction, but the style value which is essential to all smart frocks.

47

Reference Index

Relative Sizes of Needles and Thread

(Class and Variety of Needles Used, 15 x 1)

Sizes of Needles	Classes of Work	Sizes of Cotton, Silk or Linen Thread
9	Georgette, chiffon, light-weight rayon, fine dimity, lawn, batiste and other feather-weight or sheer fabrics. For infants' clothes and for dainty lingerie, also fine lace and all delicate or gossamer fabrics.	100 to 150 Cotton OO & OOO Silk Twist
11	All medium light-weight, summertime fabrics. For children's clothes, dainty house dresses and aprons, glass curtains.	80 to 100 Cotton O Silk Twist
14	Light-weight woolens, firm dress silks and cottons, draperies and fabric furnishings. For smocks and men's fine shirts. For general household sewing; for fine quilting.	60 to 80 Cotton A & B Silk Twist
16	Heavy cretonne, madras, muslin and quilts. For stitching aprons and men's work shirts. For making buttonholes.	40 to 60 Cotton C Silk Twist
18	Bed ticking, awnings, porch furniture covers, boy's duck suits.	30 to 40 Cotton D Silk Twist
19	Heavy weaves of coating, suiting, ticking, sacking, tarpaulin, duck, drilling, canvas. For wash uniforms and bedding supplies for hospitals and hotels.	24 to 30 Cotton E Silk Twist 60 to 80 Linen
21	Bags, Coarse Cloths and heavy Goods.	40 to 60 Linen or very Coarse Cotton

When sending orders for needles be sure to specify the size required.

You will obtain the best stitching results from your sewing machine if it is fitted with a Singer needle.

The Sign of
Singer Service
Throughout the World

SINGER
SEWING
MACHINES

SINGER SEWING LIBRARY—No. 3

HOW TO MAKE
CHILDREN'S
CLOTHES
The Modern Singer Way

Published by Singer Sewing Machine Co., Inc.

FOREWORD

ALL who sew for children will find delight in this book. The simple methods, practical instruction, and valuable suggestions are so arranged as to be ready for instant use.

If you are making a layette, read in its entirety the section devoted to layettes and infants' clothing. Aside from the actual instructions for making the garments, you will find just the counsel and help about the contents of a layette and the materials to use that you have been looking for.

If you are interested in making rompers or bloomer frocks, or if there is a little boy to provide clothes for, read the entire section on the subject. Then the making of any such garments will take on a new interest for you. As a result you will be able to exceed your own good expectations in creating garments that are not only appropriate, but correct from point of construction.

Clothes for school girls are always a problem, the time for cultivating good taste important. Every mother with a girl of from kindergarten to high school age will find usable information and suggestions, as well as definite instructions, that will help her in expressing both appropriate good taste and smartness in all the garments that she makes.

A girl's first party dress, her graduation dress, her middy suit for camp or country, her gymnasium suit for school—all these are items that mothers must know about. Brief, authentic information is given that will answer questions and make the creating of such garments a delight rather than a responsibility.

Modern sewing methods and a modern Singer sewing machine are essentials that combine to make sewing at home recreational and economically valuable. This book speaks the language of both in a simple, usable way.

Complete reference index on page 64

PUBLISHED BY

SINGER SEWING MACHINE CO., INC.

SINGER BUILDING, NEW YORK

PRICE 25 CENTS

Adv. No. 1976

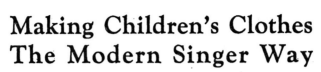

Making Children's Clothes
The Modern Singer Way

By Mary Brooks Picken

SEWING the modern way with perfected patterns, fabrics of beauty that can be bought at little cost, and a sewing machine with hidden power that responds instantly to one's wish, makes sewing recreational and intriguingly interesting. The creation of things that are both beautiful and useful is an art that women can master and enjoy.

Those privileged to plan and make clothes for children should compensate for the pleasure and satisfaction derived by determining at the very outset to make clothes that will be fully appropriate for the child and in keeping with the child's temperament and activities.

Good taste in clothes, as in conduct, comes from principles established through association and practice. The mother who knows the treasured virtue of good taste will consider it as important to cultivate good taste in clothes in her children as good manners and correct speech.

Good taste in clothes will not develop alongside of ill-chosen colors and designs, inappropriate textures, or indifferent combinations of color, line or fabric. Artistic wearing of apparel means there must be the right feeling of clothes for the purpose—play clothes designed as play clothes, school clothes as school clothes, and dress-up clothes correctly conceived for the occasions on which they are to be worn.

Children's clothes rightly designed invariably express a beautiful feeling of simplicity and are in every sense appropriate.

Cotton fabrics and machine work, the two chief factors in children's clothes, make it possible to have beautiful clothes inexpensively.

This book is designed to make sewing for children easy, to make the work interesting, and to encourage those who sew for children to appreciate the importance of correct and becoming attire, thus helping in a silent way to build a foundation of good taste and a sense of fitness for the child that will later prove an asset, economically and socially.

Cleanliness is the first requisite of attractive children. It is an asset of immeasurable importance. In planning clothes for children, think first of how many changes of clothing are necessary. Then distribute your money and sewing time in such a way as to provide abundantly.

The garments illustrated throughout this book are types that are generally in favor. You can therefore apply the instructions given and at the same time use your favorite make of pattern. The order in which the garment is assembled is important to quick results, the perfection of detail upon an understanding of approved and modern methods.

1

Fabrics and Trimmings

CHOOSE first a material that will launder easily, preferably a fabric with very little filling such as starch, which is added to give an undeserved weight and finish to the fabric. A fabric needs to be rather closely woven to give satisfactory service. This is considered from point of wear and of retaining original shape. Sleazy materials lose their shape easily and take on premature shabbiness.

Colors should be fast. "Warranted" fast color and "guaranteed" fast color have different meanings. Warranted means a fairly fast color, while guaranteed means that the manufacturer will replace the material or refund the money in case the material fades. At one time it seemed necessary to "set" colors in wash fabrics before making them up. With modern dyes and modern washing methods this is rarely necessary.

Cottons shrink from ¼ inch to 1 inch per yard in length in washing, and about half this amount in width. Bear this in mind in cutting, and finish an 18-inch skirt ¼ to ⅜ inch longer than the desired finished length; likewise the sleeves and waist.

When it is a matter of economy, both as regards money and time, buy sturdy fabrics that will stand much wear and washing. Many mothers who want real smartness and a style quality in their children's clothes see first the exclusive, expensive materials that are often imported, and then select from the less expensive fabrics, colors and designs that are in keeping with the more expensive qualities.

Cotton suiting, a fabric in imitation of linen, and made by practically every cotton manufacturer, comes in the class of *sturdy* fabrics. Its yardage cost is small, its wearing quality excellent.

Gingham is a dyed-in-the-yarn fabric, with the design running true with the warp and woof. This factor is a real aid in making garments because of the ease in cutting and the surety that it will be perfectly straight, especially for ironing.

Fabrics with designs printed on are very attractive, but it is necessary to beware of large printed designs, especially stripes, plaids and checks, as they are liable to be printed out of line with the warp and woof. This presents a serious problem in cutting, making and ironing. As a rule one should tear the fabric, or pull a thread and cut across one end of the fabric to straighten it, and begin pinning the pattern on from the straightened end.

Each season finds fashion emphasis on certain fabrics, and as a result ginghams will be more popular than prints, and again, prints more popular than ginghams, or dotted swiss preferred to organdie, crepe to piqué, etc. Most cotton manufacturers put out a "children's line" in addition to their regular line of cottons. In this line the designs are smaller and the colors pure or pastel. In buying for children always bear in mind that designs and colors appropriate for children are as important as appropriate texture.

Trimmings. Printed fabrics should, as a rule, be trimmed with a plain fabric of the same quality to insure evenness in wearing. Bias bindings make a quick, practical trimming, and are a great aid in

2

finishing. Bias bindings are used perhaps more than any other trimming for children's clothes. Ready-made bias bindings may be purchased made of percale, lawn, nainsook, organdie, and silk. In buying binding, choose that of a quality to wear evenly with the dress fabric, and be certain that the color harmonizes with the fabric or enhances it by contrast.

Ready-made bindings come in several widths. Width number 5 gives the greatest satisfaction when used in your sewing machine binder. If you prefer to make your own binding, cut it on a true bias and seam the pieces together so that your joining allows an even line on the bias edges. A bias cutting gauge that may be purchased at your sewing machine shop will serve admirably to cut evenly bias pieces of the desired width.

When you start planning garments for children, take samples of the different materials with you to the notion department of your store. There you can match threads, bindings and tapes, and find trimming braids and edges, elastic, buttons of the right size and color—all to save your time in sewing and at the same time give to the garments the evidence of thoughtful planning.

Spool cotton in colors is often effective either for contrast or to harmonize perfectly with the material. Such thread comes in three sizes— for sheer fabrics, for firmer fabrics, and in a heavy thread for decorative stitching on the machine. White thread comes in sizes 8 to 200.

For fine work use fine thread and fine needles; for coarse work, coarser thread and medium needles; for very coarse work, cretonne, denim, and overcoating, use the coarsest threads and needles. Always have your thread and needles in full accord with the texture of your fabric. This is very important if the best effects are to be obtained. (See "Relative Sizes f Needles and Threads" in your sewing machine instruction book.)

Embroidery in good taste and well done, never over done, adds attractiveness and value to dresses. Decorative stitching is also easy to accomplish with the sewing machine, as various illustrations in this book show. Lace is often used for children's clothes. When it is appropriate it can be very effective. In using lace choose that of a quality to wear with the fabric. Remember also that lace is tedious to iron, so place it in such a way that the ironing will be simple.

Plain collars, cuffs and pockets on designed fabrics, or designed fabrics on plain, make the preferred trimming. See good designs in shops and fashion magazines, especially pattern books. Know what is correct from points of fashion and good taste, and be guided in your selection of trimming, or combination of fabric and trimming, by approved practice.

3

Infants' Clothes

AUTHORITIES disagree on the quantity of garments necessary for a baby's layette, but all agree that beautiful cleanness is absolutely necessary. Therefore it is better to have plainer and less expensive garments, but to have enough to make immaculateness certain.

The following list of necessary equipment is given here as a guide in determining how many articles to provide. This list is the result of much research and many comparisons and opinions. It can, therefore, be used with complete assurance. Fewer articles than this calls for will mean more frequent washings; more will mean in some instances convenience, and in some real luxury.

The important thing in buying a layette is to have a list and follow it.

CONTENTS OF A LAYETTE

Three soft flannel bands, torn 5 inches wide and 28 inches long; 3 silk-and-wool vests; 3 to 6 dozen hemmed diapers; 3 flannel skirts, 2 inches shorter than dresses; 6 plain nainsook dresses, 21 to 27 inches long; 2 fine nainsook or batiste dresses, 22 to 28 inches long; 4 plain night dresses or kimonos, 26 to 30 inches long; 2 light-weight wool kimonos or wrappers, 28 inches long; 1 36"x45" eiderdown or soft flannel shawl piece to serve as a wrap for two months; 2 dainty sacques of cashmere, yarn, or crepe de Chine; 3 pairs of silk-and-wool hose; 3 18"x36" quilted pads, edges bound; 1 36"x45" wool blanket; 2 36"x45" fine cotton blankets; 4 36"x45" sheets; 1 rubber sheet; 2 11"x16" baby pillows (very soft); 6 fine nainsook or handkerchief linen pillow cases.

Some old, unhemmed bits or squares of soft linen for wash cloths. Some torn pieces from old nainsook night dresses or slips or from worn table cloths that are soft, for drying instead of towels when baby is very new. One piece should be large enough to wrap the baby in at birth. Such a cloth should be placed inside an old, perfectly clean, soft, wool shawl or piece of blanket.

One box baby talcum; 1 piece baby soap; 1 small package of absorbent cotton; 1 roll of sterile gauze; 1 tube or jar of white vaseline; small bottle of boric acid solution; 2 dozen small, 2 dozen medium, 2 dozen large safety pins; a little basket for supplies; a bassinet or crib.

Shoes, bootees, bibs, caps, decorated sacques, comfortables, clothes rack, hangers, and baby book are not included in the above list. These may be purchased or provided as gifts. Though desirable, they are not considered as wholly necessary.

The texture of materials for baby things is most important, and the mother must use judgment in what she buys. Infants' shirts and stockings, for example, must be fine to be soft enough and they should have the required wool for warmth. Nainsook, which is ideal for baby dresses, can be had from 2 dollars a yard down to 10 cents a yard; so the mother herself must judge what quality she will buy. A good quality that will launder nicely and be soft and delicate enough for baby, can be had for from 35 to 80 cents a yard. This quality is usually best for two reasons: it lasts longer in laundering, and there is such little yardage required for each garment that one can afford to buy a nice quality. The same is true of flannel petticoats. So often a woman may choose an inferior grade of flannel, not realizing what a tiny bit it takes to make a garment, and feeling that $1.25 to $1.75 a yard is too much to pay for such a fabric. But when she realizes that three little petticoats can, by careful placing of pattern pieces, be made from 2¼ to 2½ yards, it is not so expensive. This point holds true also of fleeced cottons, of challis and silks appropriate for baby. The yardage is so small that a satisfactory quality is not expensive.

4

Sewing for Infants

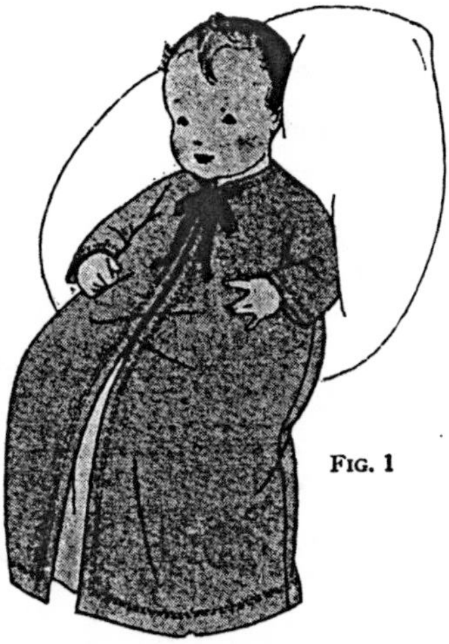

FIG. 1

THE important thing in starting to sew dainty things is to equip the sewing basket at the outset with fine cotton sewing thread. There should be fine needles and dainty edgings, fine bindings and tapes—all dainty enough to belong to baby and delicate enough to be appropriate to the garments that you make. When you are shopping, buy the essentials in notions so that they will be at hand when you are ready to sew.

It is best to buy a 10-yard piece of fine nainsook and use this for dresses and slips, and buy a bolt or bolts of diaper cloth, if diapers are to be cut and hemmed at home. Buy the necessary yardage for all the flannel petticoats because they cut to so much better advantage when three are cut at one time.

When you have assembled a goodly portion of the things with which you wish to sew, have your patterns at hand. Measure the patterns and decide the length you wish the dresses and slips to be. The dresses should be in every case two inches longer than the slips. If the pattern is too long, fold in tucks to get the right length, and then proceed to cut out several dresses or several slips at one time. Assemble the parts of each dress, decide how you are going to trim it, and make a little bundle, complete in itself. When the dresses are all cut, take one by one from the stock, finish it completely, and put it in with the baby supplies. Tiny garments can grow like magic when such a plan is carried out.

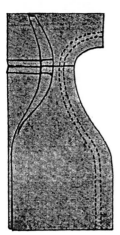

FIG. 2

Cut lining and outside exactly alike, seam separately, and press seams open. Place right sides together. Stitch all the way around, leaving lower edges of sleeves open. Turn right side out and whip bottom of sleeves. Machine stitching ¾ inch in, and ⅛ in. apart, as shown, trims all edges.

For a kimono finished with facings rather than a lining, cut the facings to fit, stitch all around the edges, and clip the seams. Turn the facings to the right side and stitch them on both edges. French seam the under-arms and put a 1-inch hem in the bottom.

FIG. 3

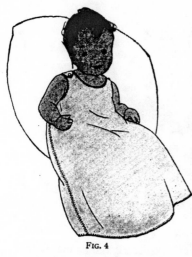

FIG. 4

Cutting Out. When you have opened up your patterns and read the description of each garment, separated them and pinned the parts of each pattern together, it is wise to put each pattern in an envelope by itself so that you can have it ready when you want to cut the slips, or dresses, or petticoats. All patterns usually allow for ⅜-inch seams. If you are using very fine nainsook, lawn or batiste for the dresses, and making French seams, perhaps you will want to trim the seams of your pattern a little bit, making them ¼-inch instead of ⅜. This is especially desirable in making collar edges and sleeve bands, because the daintier seams are more in keeping with baby garments.

Arrange your cutting out so that you will have garments of different kinds ready to sew. If you feel like making a little slip some afternoon, the slip will be all ready to sew and it will not be necessary for you to arrange a cutting surface and get out your cutting equipment. Label each little package as you fold it up and mark on it just what you intend to do with it, so that when you begin to sew a garment you will not have to think about what you planned to do with it when cutting it.

Machine Work. Many women exclaim regretfully when they see machine stitching on a baby's garment. But there are no regrets if one takes the precaution to buy fine sewing thread and uses a fine needle and short sewing stitch. It is a fault only when one forgets to change the needle and the thread, and uses thread and needle that are in keeping with regular household articles or adult garments.

Many of the finest baby dresses that are French seamed have the first seams stitched on the machine and the second seams done by hand. This is an ideal way because the machine stitching gives strength to the seam and allows it to hold better in laundering, and to all appearances the dress is entirely hand made. Any French seam, however, can be done beautifully by machine. Fine tucks can be put in by machine and then the tucks pulled crosswise gently to give a hand hemstitched effect.

FIG. 5

6

Making Baby Slips

Flannel Slips. The simplest yet most necessary slip is the flannel one in Fig. 4. This should be plain and made to button on the shoulders.

Cut the slip out, stitch the side seams and press them open, and cat-stitch the raw edges back as in Fig. 6. The outside edges may be basted for hemstitching, sent to the hemstitching shop, and all edges machine hemstitched. Cut the edges away up to within ⅛ inch of the hemstitching, but not through the center. The edges may be left thus, as in Fig. 7, or you may crochet with single stitches through the holes made by the hemstitching. When this is done with No. 100 mercerized crochet thread it gives a very satisfactory, smooth finish which is both decorative and serviceable.

If the climate is very warm the upper part of the flannel slip may be made of firm nainsook. Babies born in the winter or early spring usually need slips all of flannel, even in moderate climates.

If a nainsook yoke is used or substituted later for the flannel top, simply hem the edges by machine and join the yoke to the flannel skirt.

Cotton Slips. To make the nainsook slip as in Fig. 5, cut according to the pattern, French seam the shoulder and under-arm seams, and face the neck and armholes, as in Fig. 8, using for this a true bias facing cut a scant ⅝ inch wide. Stitch the facing on, on the right side, turn it back to the wrong side, trim the seam to ⅛ inch all the way around, turn the raw edge in, and stitch it neatly to place.

Join the ruffle pieces together, using a plain, pressed-open seam. With the machine hemmer, hem the lower edge; then put two tiny tucks the width of the hem above the hem, spacing them ⅜ to ½ inch apart. Gather the top edge of the ruffle, using the Ruffler and join it to the slip, stitching it in a narrow French seam on the right side made in width to harmonize with the tucks in the ruffle. Place two tucks above this seam in the skirt, as in Fig. 9, thus completing the slip. Groups of 5 or 7 tucks may be used, or 5 in the ruffle and 3 above. Too many tucks make unnecessary work and are tedious to iron. The right amount serves all purposes admirably.

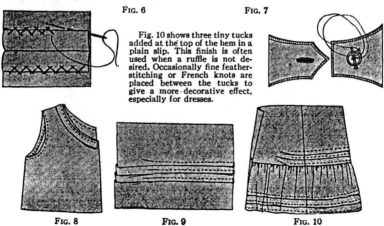

FIG. 6   FIG. 7

Fig. 10 shows three tiny tucks added at the top of the hem in a plain slip. This finish is often used when a ruffle is not desired. Occasionally fine feather-stitching or French knots are placed between the tucks to give a more decorative effect, especially for dresses.

FIG. 8   FIG. 9   FIG. 10

7

Bishop Dresses

Fig. 11

THE most practical and popular baby dress, shown in Fig. 11, is the bishop, or raglan sleeve, dress. This provides a roomy armhole and is slightly easier to make than a dress with a set-in sleeve.

French seam the armholes, hem the neck and sleeve edges with the foot hemmer, which makes the narrowest machine hem, and make a hemmed placket for the back closing, as in Fig. 12. Some stitch a narrow tuck on the wrong side of the neck and sleeves ¾ inch in from the edges, then run a fine crocheted chain through the tucks. The tape can be drawn up and tied in bows for wearing, yet opened out for ironing. Another alternative is to gather the edges ¾ inch in and stitch very narrow tape directly under the gathering, this serving to hold the fulness permanently in place. When this is done, make a loop of the tape on the lapping edge at the back neck, the loop serving as a buttonhole, as in Fig. 12.

French seam the under-arm seams, stitching from the wrist edge up to the armhole and then down to the bottom of the dress. Put the hem in with tucks at the top, as explained for a slip, Fig. 10.

Variations of the Bishop Dress. The neck and sleeve edges may be bound and left plain, or narrow baby lace may be sewed or crocheted to the edges. (The best lace for baby clothes is a dainty, washable lace from ⅛ to ¼ inch wide and called in the trade "baby lace.") A ruffle may be added to the lower edge rather than a hem. Several rows of tucks and insertion may be used in decorating either a plain edge or a ruffled edge. A dainty embroidery design may ornament either the center of the front yoke portion, the left shoulder of the dress, or each sleeve ¼ of the way up from the wrist, or embroidery decoration may be used at the top of the hem in front or all the way around.

Dainty materials and available time often make possible interesting and unusual finishes that add value and charm to such an otherwise simple little dress.

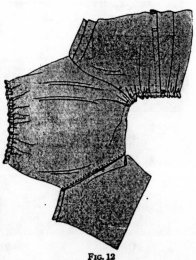

Fig. 12

Tucked Yoke Dresses

Fig. 13

BABY dresses should have some fulness provided, either by means of gathers, tucks, or yoke fulness.

Tucking is very practical, especially when machine made, and may be put in in groups of two, three, four and five, as many as desired. In any event make the tucks tiny enough to insure daintiness.

In making a dress such as Fig. 13, decide first on the space the tucks will occupy in width and depth. The front of an infant's dress will measure 8 to 8½ inches across. The depth of a tucked yoke should not exceed 3½ inches from the shoulder down.

Adjust the tucker so that the markings and spacings will be correct for the space that the tucks will occupy. Put in all the tucks before you shape the yoke. Take care in doing this to place the first tuck in the tucker on a lengthwise thread. In this way all the tucks will come in a true line with the warp.

The simplest way to cut such a dress is to measure the width of the dress at the lower edge. 50 to 54 inches is the usual width when the material is fine. If the material is slightly heavier, a skirt 48 inches around is correct.

When the width for the bottom of the skirt has been decided upon, fold your material lengthwise ¼ this distance from the selvage. Use the fold as a center front and center back line and tuck on each side of it to make the yoke portion. The detail of tucks and yoke, Fig. 14, shows how the tucks are first grouped, the threads pulled through to the wrong side and tied, and then how the pattern is put on and the yoke shaped.

Many patterns allow a plait at the under-arm as shown opened out in Fig. 15 and closed in Fig. 19 on the opposite page. As in Fig. 15, the outside lines are brought together, meeting at the center line, and thus giving an inverted plait made just deep enough to fit the lower part of the armhole.

The back of the dress, with tucks at each side of the back opening, is shown in Fig. 15. When the yoke and armhole edges are shaped, French seam the shoulder and under-arm seams and put the hem in. The inverted plait at the under-arm allows of a straighter under-arm seam and therefore a straighter hem. A plain hem 3 to 5 inches deep is usually desirable with a tucked yoke. A tucked or ruffled lower edge would be contrary in design and therefore undesirable for a dress such as this.

The sleeves have a ⅜-inch finished band at the lower edge with baby lace sewed to the edge.

The tiny collar pieces, because of their curves, have narrow hems

9

basted first, then the lace sewed on, which makes one row of stitching suffice for hem and lace. Those expert in using the hemmer turn the hem and sew the lace on with one operation. A rolled hem may be used, the edge rolled and the lace whipped on at the same time, or the raw edge may be turned once and stitched, then the lace whipped on. The whipping stitching pulls the raw edge in enough to conceal it.

Stitch the sleeves with French seams and then French seam them in position in the armholes. Pin the collar pieces in place on the neck and sew them with a very narrow bias facing which conceals all raw edges.

In finishing neck edges for infants' clothes, remember that little necks are short, and that the under-shirt usually comes up close to the neck, which makes it necessary for collars to be flat and without any bulk in the band or facing. Seams should be very smooth and facings perfectly flat so that they will not rub or irritate. The buttons in the back should be small and flat so that they will not be uncomfortable. Usually one button at the neck and one at the placket opening are sufficient.

Often in using 36-inch material for baby dresses a width and a half are used for a dress, the half width coming in the back, the seams arranged to come at the under-fold of the inverted plait. When this plan is followed, seam the material together first; then put what is left of the skirt fulness in the under-arm plaits. A plain dress pattern will serve in cutting the dress in correct proportions.

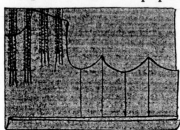

FIG. 14. Make the tucks even at the lower edge, using a pin to pull the stitching back. Pull the threads to the wrong side and tie the two threads at the end of each tuck. Take care to avoid tightening.

FIG. 16. Avoid stretching the curved edges. Allow the lace to ease in on a curve so that it will be flat. The firm thread at the top of the lace can often be drawn up to serve as a gathering thread.

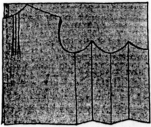

FIG. 15. Finish the end of the tucks, lap the placket and pin it in correct position. Place the pattern on, center back of pattern to center back lengthwise fold of dress.

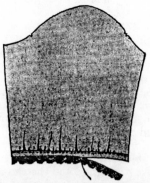

FIG. 17. Adjust the gathers evenly, keeping them, toward the center of the sleeve. When practical, finish the wrist edge before stitching the under-arm seam.

Square Yoke Dresses

ONE square yoke dress at least is in every baby's wardrobe, both its simplicity and its possibilities for ornamentation making it a very desirable type.

The construction of the square yoke dress is considered here more than its possible variations of tucking, embroidering, hemstitching, or insertion inserts, because when trimming is used, it is invariably put in before the yoke is cut, therefore making the decoration a simple matter and the construction the important one.

FIG. 18

In cutting sections for a baby's garment cut on the true lengthwise grain wherever possible. The slightest error in grain, or any irregularity in cutting, shows conspicuously in so tiny a garment as a baby's dress.

In developing the dress in Fig. 18, finish the under-arm seams first, then gather the front and back of the skirt of the dress at the top. If the material frays easily, and the yoke is to be joined with lace insertion, it is a good idea to hem the edge, using a long machine stitch, then to draw the thread up, thus making the hemming thread serve as a gathering thread. When this is done it is advisable to use a number 80 thread rather than 120, which is generally recommended for baby clothes.

When the gathering is finished, the yoke and skirt portions are joined. In this case a narrow lace insertion finely woven, but of durable thread, is used.

Fig. 19 shows the method of assembling the dress by means of insertion; also how the inverted under-arm plait is held to place with stitching. Put the insertion in, then hem and finish the back lapped placket.

Finish the bottom of the skirt with plain or decorated hem. Finish the sleeves and insert them in the armholes, the insertion serving to join them in the same way as the yoke and skirt were joined. A narrow hem finishes the neck, to which narrow matching lace is stitched.

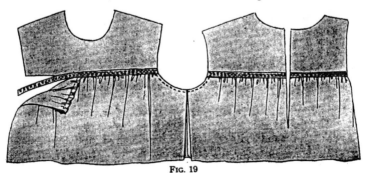

FIG. 19

11

Round Yoke Dresses

Fig. 20

A FAVORED baby dress, one especially preferred in hand made dresses, is the round yoke dress. It is slightly more tedious to make than the bishop, tucked, or square yoke dress. It is, however, so babyish and attractive that one or two in the layette are well worth any tediousness experienced in making.

The chief precaution is to gather the fulness in the back and front of the dress, as in Figs. 21 and 22, so that the edges can meet without crowding or stretching. The center front of the yoke is usually cut on a lengthwise thread, the shoulder and center back coming on a bias grain.

Finish the under-arm seams with a French seam. Stitch the inverted plait to position. Shirr in the front and back of the yoke portions and complete the yoke, as shown in Fig. 23; then join the yoke and skirt by pinning both together, placing the pins crosswise as close as 1½ inches apart. When the yoke is pinned it is easy to make sure of the perfection of the joining, and also that the dress portion hangs correctly from the yoke. Replace the pins with basting and then replace the basting with machine stitching. The raw seam may be turned back and whipped down by hand, or a second row of machine stitching may be added to the center of the insertion to hold the edge of the seam. This is advisable only when the insertion is finely enough woven and close enough in pattern to prevent the raw edge from showing.

Entre deux, or veining, which may be purchased by the yard, is often used in joining square or round yokes to skirts. This is like machine hemstitching embroidered over. It usually has a lawn or batiste edge on each side. This extra material is used in seaming the entre deux to place, its surplus width trimmed away. Then the yoke and skirt are whipped to the entre deux, the stitches taken from the right side and directly through the holes, as shown in Fig. 27.

The hemmed placket and back shirring for the round yoke dress are shown in Fig. 22. Fig. 24 shows how the gathering thread under the insertion in the sleeve is put in, and how the lace and insertion are applied. Fig. 25 shows how the lower edge of the sleeve may be bound and lace added, in the event that a simpler sleeve is desired than Fig. 24 shows.

Fig. 26 shows an interesting hem, one frequently used for infants' dresses. The top edge of the hem is scalloped, the edges turned in, the corners clipped off and the top edge stitched, each point turned precisely on the point to make a perfect scallop. Such a hem may be put in with a heavier thread, a medium size crochet cotton serving admirably. When

12

this is used, have the sewing machine needle large enough to carry the thread. The hem may also be held to place with French knots or feather-stitching. The scallops may be turned to the right or wrong side. Lace or piping may be used at the top of the scallops. For older children, two or three rows of machine stitching may be used for the top. This kind of hem is just as appropriate for a graduation frock as it is for a christening robe, the size of the scallop and the method of finishing in each case suiting the size of the garment and texture of the material.

Round yoke dresses are often used for little girls two and three years old. In such cases the fulness is usually held in with smocking. Outline stitches are sometimes used over machine shirrings to give a smocked effect.

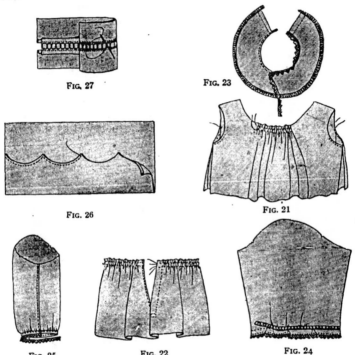

FIG. 27

FIG. 23

FIG. 26

FIG. 21

FIG. 25   FIG. 22   FIG. 24

FIG. 21. Adjust the fulness evenly by pulling gently crosswise of the gathering lines. If the material stretches easily, run a stitching line all around the edge one-eighth inch in from the edge, to hold it to shape preparatory to joining the yoke.

FIG. 22. Placket opening plus yoke should measure at least 8 inches to allow the dress to be put on easily.

FIG. 23. Because of the bias hem in the center back it is sometimes necessary to stitch a lengthwise piece of the material inside the hem, to serve as a stay for buttons and buttonholes.

FIG. 24. Measure the insert 6 to 7 inches.

Gather the sleeve top and bottom, to fit, placing most of the fulness at center.

FIG. 25. Clip the first seam close to the stitching at the wrist to avoid bulk in the second seam. Stitch back on the seam to secure it.

FIG. 26. Clip the curves of the scallops one-eighth inch in and turn the edge with regard to line so that the shape of the scallop will be retained. Lift the presser foot and pivot the needle at each point of the scallops so that an exact turn will be made.

FIG. 27. Stitch the seam on the veining to the dress. Use one raw edge as a seam finish, turning it under. Use whipping stitches to hold the edges.

13

FIG. 28

Layette Accessories

A BABY sacque is desirable from the standpoint of warmth if the baby is frequently taken up, especially as soon as he begins to sit up. The simplest butterfly type of sacque, as in Fig. 28, will be found very practicable and easy to make and iron. The garment is cut all in one piece. It may be made of light weight wool or silk. The edges may be bound, blanket stitched, machine stitched, hemmed, faced, or hemstitched.

The sacque illustrated is made of light weight, pale pink albatross. Have the edges hemstitched all the way around, trim the edges away up to the hemstitching line, the same as for the flannel slip, page 7, and crochet through the holes made by the hemstitching. These holes provide also openings through which narrow tie ribbon may be slipped to form fastenings for the under-arm and center front, or the edges may be whipped together with the knitting silk at the points indicated by the bows. A tie may also be made of a crocheted chain of the thread. When double it is quite attractive. Several such sacques are pleasing and useful in a layette. They have a dress-up air about them that mothers like, and they have the advantage of warmth.

In binding the edges of a sacque, use binding narrower than number 5, and take the precaution to make two rows of machine stitching to prevent the binding from pulling away. With the two rows of stitching the binder is not used because the binding is first stitched on as a facing and then brought over to the right side, the edge turned in, and stitched as a binding. The last turn of the binding may be held to place with French knots or dainty stitches. In such a case, first put the tie ribbons to place so that the binding or edge finish will conceal their joining. When the edges are blanket stitched, turn the raw edge in as a narrow hem and stitch it, using fine matching thread. When the blanket stitching is placed over this the hem with its stitching line will be almost entirely concealed. The edges may be machine stitched, the same as for the kimono, Fig. 1. In such a case, use a lining for the sacque and stitch all the way around the garment. Then turn it right side out and add decorative stitching to hold the lining and outside together. A kimono and sacque, finished alike, make a very attractive gift set.

FIG. 29. In binding baby blankets, if a miter is to be made, pin it in as you turn the corner so that ample length will be allowed. Clip the blanket corner as shown to avoid bulk.

14

Baby Coats

Some mothers use a kimono pattern and make a simple, plain coat of white wool. Others prefer to take the kimono pattern and add a cape, such as is shown here. Others use a shawl or blanket for the baby's first wrap rather than make a coat. A coat, however, seems an essential part of the baby's dress-up things. If made large enough at the beginning it may serve for the first nine months, possibly a whole year.

The coat in Fig. 30 is a dress-up type. The scalloped cape and cuffs, the yoke shirrings, the decorative stitching and pearl buttons make the ornamentation. To make such a coat, cut the lining the same as the coat except for the allowance for the facings or hems on the coat.

FIG. 30

Seam the under-arm seams of the coat and lining. Place the wrong sides together and stitch the lining to the front edges of the coat. Then proceed with the shirring as in Fig. 31, gathering through both the coat and lining. To do this simply lengthen the stitch, loosen the tension slightly, and with the presser foot as a guide put in the required number of straight stitching rows. Gather these up by pulling all the bottom threads. Slip the material along on the threads until the shirrings are all uniform. When the shirrings are drawn up to correspond in spacing with the bottom of the front yoke, pull the thread ends through to the wrong side, thread a needle with them, and secure each row with several fine whipping stitches.

Stitch the shoulder seams of the yoke and lining and put in the bound buttonholes, as in Fig. 32. First mark the position of the buttonhole, then place a piece of material, four times larger than the buttonhole is to be, over the buttonhole position. Stitch it in, oblong box effect, as at *a*. Make a slash inside this and clip the ends fork fashion to allow a flat turn. Clip exactly to the stitched line, but not through it. Pull the piece to the wrong side as at *b* and shape it to place to form a welt as at *c*. Baste the welt accurately, then whip the raw edges down on the wrong side, taking care that the stitches do not show on the right.

Baste and stitch the skirt part of the coat to the bottom edge of the yoke. Whip the lining down over this. Fig. 33 shows how the lining and yoke are basted together before the lining is whipped, to make sure that it will not draw at any place. Make the cape and cuffs next. If the edges are to be scalloped as shown, place the right sides of the material and lining together, and baste the outside edges 2½ inches in from the edge. This will hold the lining and material together and make the marking of the scallops easier. If you are using a transfer pattern that has scallops, simply pin the pattern to the lining side of the cape and make

15

the transfer. If you are marking the scallops with a cup or round object, begin at the corners and work up and back, as in going around the cape it may be necessary to make the scallops slightly smaller or larger to have them fit in exactly. When the scallops are marked, stitch precisely on the scalloped line, as in Fig. 34. Trim away to a seam's width the surplus material outside the scallops, and clip the points of each scallop up to the stitching line, but never across it. Remove the basting and turn the cape right side out. With the fingers shape the scallops perfectly. Sometimes the top of a wire hairpin run along the seam on the right side will bring the edge out to line quickly. After the scallops are pressed from the right side, baste them in preparation for one or two rows of decorative stitching which may be added, as in Fig. 30. This stitching has a two-fold purpose in that it decorates and at the same time holds the lining to position.

Stitch the sleeves and their linings separately and put them together so that their pressed open seams are inside. Bring the edges together at the wrist, place the cuff to position and catch all edges in with a bias facing. Stitch this on the right side, turn it to the wrong side, and fell it to the lining. Stitch the sleeves in the armholes, catching the coat and lining of the sleeve into the armhole of the coat. Bring the lining of the coat down and fell it over the seam, thus concealing it.

Join the cape to the coat with a bias facing, which thus completes the neck-line. Hem the lower edge of the coat and the lining separately, as in Fig. 35. This makes the coat much easier to press. If no lining is used in the skirt portion of the coat, stitch on each side of the seam, as in Fig. 36, to hold the raw edges of the seams to place. Remove all bastings and thread ends, press the coat, and sew the buttons on.

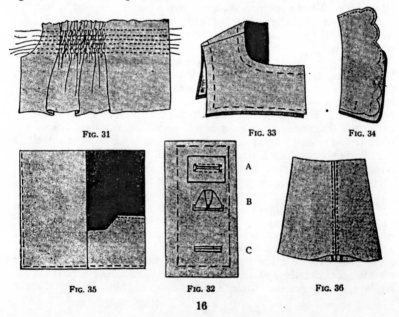

FIG. 31   FIG. 33   FIG. 34

A

B

C

FIG. 35   FIG. 32   FIG. 36

16

Miscellaneous Equipment

Diapers. In making diapers, pull a thread and cut them so that they will be straight. Tearing such material usually frays the edges, making it necessary to trim them before hemming. Hem diapers by machine, using the foot hemmer. Hem a number at one time, and when all are stitched, remove the hemmer, and with the presser foot in place reenforce the corners by stitching back and forth on them twice for a distance of 2 or 3 inches. Diapers are so frequently washed that only sturdy corners will withstand the wear. For the same reason number 50 thread is practical in hemming them.

Bands. Most physicians and nurses prefer bands of flannel with the edges torn rather than hemmed, to prevent irritation, as a band to function must be lapped and pinned rather snugly. Some prefer fine nainsook bands made double, the seams clipped so that they cannot tighten. Occasionally darts are put in bands, placed 2 inches each side of the crosswise center, and are made ½ inch deep, tapering to nothing at the center of the band. The darts should be cut and pressed open. Because bands are worn for only a few weeks, they are made simple, without any elaboration or decoration. Safety pins are preferred to tie tapes because the size may be more easily regulated.

Shirts. Shirts should not be made at home because of the need of flat, smooth seams. Knitted garments accomplish this more easily than seamed ones. Many authorities prefer double front shirts that lap across the abdomen, believing that they give warmth and support where needed.

Bassinets. Bassinets may be purchased ready made or may be made at home. A practical one is made by covering a latticed clothes or merchandise basket. The shallow, large-sized baskets with a sturdy handle at each end are best. Place newspapers in the bottom of the basket and then pad with cotton batting which has been covered with cheesecloth. This padding should line the entire basket, the sides as well as the bottom. Sometimes a regulation pillow can be put in the bottom of the basket for additional softness.

When the padding and lining are complete, make a ruffle for the outside edge, using for this dotted Swiss, batiste, soft rayon or silk. The ruffle may be trimmed with tucks, tiny ruffles, lace insertion, binding or lace edging. It is a good idea to see attractive bassinets in the shops and then to create one that meets your idea of appropriate good taste. When a fabric such as dotted Swiss or batiste is used for the ruffle, often pale pink or blue silkaline is used underneath to give a delicate color effect. In such cases, a bow of wide soft ribbon, or rosettes of narrow ribbon, in the same color, may be fastened to the outside. The handles, if they protrude, should be wrapped with ribbon.

Removable sheets and baby pillows with their slips complete the inside. Monogrammed sheets and pillow cases are attractive for bassinets and cribs. These may be stamped and hand embroidered, or ready-made initials can be purchased and applied with hand embroidery.

17

Rompers

INFANTS' clothes are usually designed to be entirely sufficient for the first nine months to one year. When the dresses are made short at first, they need not be shortened when the baby starts to creep or stand alone. Rompers are often made to supplement the first clothes, the better dresses still serving for dress-up and the rompers coming into use for every day. Rompers may be made of white or delicate colors, especially pale pink or blue. The first rompers are worn over the shirt, diaper and slip, and must therefore be roomy enough in the lower part to be comfortable.

First rompers differ very little for boys and girls. For instance, Figs. 37 and 38 show types simple and appropriate for either. A romper as simple as Fig. 37 offers many opportunities for variation. Buster Brown collars, or a round or square collarless neck-line may be used. For little girls a tiny ruffle at the neck, sleeves, and bottom of the pocket is attractive. Trimming pieces bound or made of contrasting material, especially white on delicately colored rompers, are appealing. Two pockets may be used instead of one, and the sleeves may be short or long. In this case the one pocket has an embroidery design outlined with machine stitching. The construction of the type of garment should be understood. Once you are familiar with it, you can vary it to suit.

To make the romper shown in Fig. 37, French seam the shoulder, under-arm and sleeve seams. Put the hems for the elastic in the legs. Apply the crotch finishing pieces as in Fig. 40. Bind the sleeves, pocket, front neck opening and collar. Pin the collar to place and put it on with a true bias facing. Sew a loop of fine woven tape at the neck to use for buttoning. Close the lower opening with buttonholes and buttons.

The overall romper in Fig. 38 is decidedly practical from the standpoint of making and ironing. The neck and each side may be bound complete with the machine binder, making the construction the simplest possible. The leg portions and belt unbutton for ironing. Bind the pockets, starting at the tops. Begin to bind the neck at the left shoulder, continue around, and overlap the binding at the joining. Catch the binding down at this point with whipping stitches.

If the material used is not firm, it is a good idea to put an extra piece of material underneath the buttons and buttonholes in the leg portion to give strength. As will be seen in Fig. 42 the hem is put across the lower part of the back waist and then folded over and darts put in to draw the waist-line a little closer. Folded-in darts are placed in the trouser portion, before the band is stitched on.

The romper in Fig. 39 is a type especially suited to sturdy children—boys and girls who look best in plain, tailored clothes. The fulness in the body part, made possible by the yoke, allows of a shaped crotch opening and a knee band. In making this romper, put three rows of machine shirring across the front. French seam the shoulder, bind the center front opening, and put the collar on with a facing. Stitch the side seams, join the romper part to the yoke, put the sleeves in. Finish the crotch and put the bands on the legs and lastly the buttons and buttonholes.

18

| FIG. 37 | FIG. 38 | FIG. 39 |

Shirrings. There are three ways to make shirrings—by hand, with a long stitch on the sewing machine, and with the ruffler attachment. In making any kind of shirring, be careful that the weight of the thread corresponds with the weight of the fabric. If put in by hand, mark the shirring position exactly with creases or with marking of pins or tracing. Often the machine gauge or presser foot marks the spacings for gathers, or the tucker may be used without the needle in place, simply to indicate by creasing the line where the shirring is to come.

Always tie the thread ends at the beginning of the shirrings. At the termination, pull the threads through to the wrong side, draw them up so that the shirrings occupy the correct space and tie on the wrong side, or sew them securely so that they will hold to place.

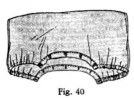

Fig. 40

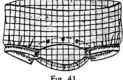

Fig. 41

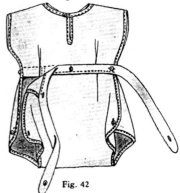

Fig. 42

FIG. 40. Put a ½-inch hem in for the elastic and stitch a crosswise piece of material cut 2 inches wide across the front of the crotch. Finish the back with a 1-inch bias facing piece. When the crotch finishings are put on they should catch the edges of the elastic at the knee, thus holding them.

FIG. 41. Use a bias piece of the material to face both edges of the crotch. When these are put to place, apply the leg bands with their piping at the upper edge. Have an extension of 1 inch on the front of the bands so that they will not be tight when buttoned.

FIG. 42. Bind the back neck opening and then continue around the neck, allowing a loop of the binding to extend out to make a fastening for the button. Tack the under-arm sections together from the belt line up to 2 or 3 inches.

19

Sun Suits and Play Clothes

THE pattern books show many attractive designs for sun suits and play clothes. Such garments are smart for children and easy to launder. Any gay prints, appropriate in design for children, may be used. The sun suit at the left is of checked percale; the overalls and hat at the right are of poplin. These are all made entirely by machine.

Pink and white print with white piqué trimming is used for Fig. 43. The apron opens down the back. A belt three-quarters of an inch wide extends from the side seams and laps and buttons at the center back. To make the apron: first, insert the 1½-inch crosswise piece of piqué at the center front, making ⅜-inch seams. Press down the material along this piece to form an ⅛-inch tuck on each side. (This allows just ¾ inch of the piqué insert to show.) Shape the crosswise bands of piqué to fit the neck and armholes, cutting them ⅞ inch wide so that when ¼-inch seams are taken on each side they will be ⅜ inch when finished. Pipe the lower edge of the front waist with crosswise piqué, put the plaits in, join the waist and skirt, stitch the shoulder seams. Apply the bands to neck and armholes, make belt pieces and place in position at under-arm seam.

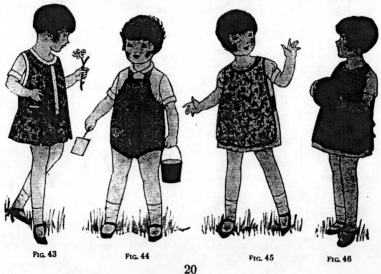

FIG. 43   FIG. 44   FIG. 45   FIG. 46

20

Stitch the under-arm seams up and put the 1 inch hem in the bottom of the apron. Lastly stitch the ¾ inch hems up each back piece.

The play overalls, Fig. 44, suitable for boys and girls, serve admirably as a semi-romper. The straps cross in the back and fasten to the front bib. These are stayed by a selvage piece 1 inch wide which has its raw edges held in with the binding across the top and at the corners.

The apron, Fig. 45, is a miniature of one mother can wear. It has a full shaped front and a back that extends down to the waist-line. Fig. 48 shows how the hem is first turned on the side back piece. The binding begins at the side and is stitched on all the way around the apron. Loops of the binding are made and placed exactly in line with the buttons which are sewed to the hems at the sides. If the loops are made and stitched to place, the binding may be done without interruption, and the first stitching, which insures security for the loops, will be entirely concealed. The pockets are bound across the top, the ends turned in, and the seam stitched all the way around. In starting to stitch the pocket on, begin ½ inch below the binding, then down and around the pocket, and through the binding on the opposite side. Turn and stitch back across the binding, thus staying the pocket at each end. Complete the apron by binding the neck.

The apron in Fig. 49 is cut in eight pieces—front, back, two shoulder straps, and four ties. The ties are shaped at the ends. The back ones are slightly shorter than the front ones. When tied these produce what is termed a "rabbit ear bow." Fig. 49 shows how the shoulder pieces are bound and placed before the apron edges are finished. The binding is used to give a waist-line effect and to relieve the plainness of the front.

FIG. 48. When the binding is complete, turn the starting end in and whip it down, as shown below. In using bias binding for loops, stitch the edges together; then place the stitched edges together when forming the loops.

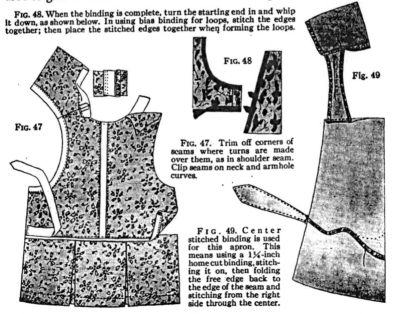

FIG. 48

Fig. 49

FIG. 47

FIG. 47. Trim off corners of seams where turns are made over them, as in shoulder seam. Clip seams on neck and armhole curves.

FIG. 49. Center stitched binding is used for this apron. This means using a 1¼-inch home cut binding, stitching it on, then folding the free edge back to the edge of the seam and stitching from the right side through the center.

21

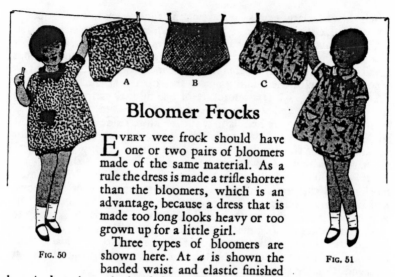

Bloomer Frocks

EVERY wee frock should have one or two pairs of bloomers made of the same material. As a rule the dress is made a trifle shorter than the bloomers, which is an advantage, because a dress that is made too long looks heavy or too grown up for a little girl.

Three types of bloomers are shown here. At *a* is shown the banded waist and elastic finished leg. At *b* we have the banded bloomer, cut on a true bias in one piece. This has side seams only and is finished with bias bound legs. As the legs may be machine bound before the side seams are stitched, this is the easiest to make. The elastic top bloomer, as shown at *c*, is not quite as comfortable as the others because of the elastic waist-line.

The making of bloomers simply and satisfactorily should be mastered at the very outset because girls wear bloomers from romper time until they are twelve or fourteen years of age. When you have a good pattern at hand and have adopted a plan of making, the task is easy.

A few things to remember about making all bloomers are: that the back should be slightly longer than the front, that there must be ample fulness in the leg and crotch, that elastics should be made to fit the leg and not too tight or loose, that bands and elastics should fit the waist-line comfortably. Use French seams in sewing the bloomers. Bind the placket openings and leave an opening in the hem at the leg seam for elastic. Buttonholes in the center of the bands are cut crosswise; at the sides, lengthwise.

FIG. 50

FIG. 51

FIG. 52

FIG. 53

FIG. 54

FIG. 52. Frocks 50 and 51 are cut from the same patterns, the trimming only making the difference. The pocket in Fig. 52 shows a binding of the dress material used as trimming.

FIG. 53. Bring the cuff ends together on the top of the sleeve. Stitch the facing to place under the turned back cuff, joining the facing one inch in front of the under-arm seam to avoid bulk at the joining.

FIG. 54. Join the elastic inside the hem. This applies to either waist-line or leg elastics. Sew the open hem down after the elastic is in place.

22

Pantie Frocks

Frocks and bloomers made for girls two to six years old are frequently called "pantie frocks" rather than "bloomer dresses", which is the name given such costumes worn by girls eight to twelve years old.

A mother will quickly decide on a type of dress most becoming to her little girl and will cling to the type, varying the coloring, the fabric and the trimming to suit her own ideas of good taste and becomingness.

The frocks shown in Figs. 50 and 51 have many possible variations. For instance, a ruffle could be used for the collar and cuff edges or for the skirt part of the dress. If a ruffle is used to trim the collar and cuffs, then the skirt part is made plain; and vice versa. Tucks may be used at the lower edge for plain fabrics, and applied bands of plain material when the dress is figured. A dress may have long or short sleeves or no sleeves, this point governed by weather, season and fashion.

The dress shown in Fig. 55 is the same as the dresses in Figs. 50 and 51. The difference lies in the method of trimming and the shape of the collar and cuffs. A ruffle hemmed with the foot hemmer and gathered with the gatherer, panels the front of the dress and edges the collar and cuffs, giving the dress a wholly different appearance.

The tucks shown in Fig. 56 serve two purposes—that of construction lines and that of ornamentation. The tucks, placed crosswise in the front and back yoke, shape both the yoke and the sleeves. The tucks at the bottom of the skirt give balance to the design. Organdie, swiss, crisp lawn or rayon is appropriate in fabric for this type of dress.

The shirred or smocked front dress, shown in Fig. 57, is opposite in effect to that of Fig. 56. Voile, crepe, challis or batiste, or any limp fabric that is not bulky, is suitable. When the shirring or smocking is put in and the fullness adjusted as desired, cut the dress from a plain pattern. A 4-inch hem is more appropriate for a plain dress such as this than the regulation 2½ inch hem used for pantie frocks. The neck of this type of frock may be round or square. Again, a collar and long sleeves may be used. For the shirring or smocking the thread used may be of a color to match the binding of the dress, especially if the color is not deep. A plain back with a hemmed placket opening may be used, or the back may be made the same as the front. In such a case, make the dress to slip over the head and without an opening.

FIG. 55   FIG. 56   FIG. 57

23

Decorative Stitching

TRIMSTITCH is a decorative thread, right in size and texture for use on the sewing machine. It is admirable for children's clothes as it decorates as you sew. Simply use No. 18 machine needle—one that will take size 20 thread. Use Trimstitch on top and bottom for all decorative stitching and size 24 white six-cord cotton thread on the bobbin for smocking or shirring. Lengthen the machine stitch to make from seven to nine stitches to the inch, depending on the material, then proceed just as with ordinary machine stitching. At the termination of the stitching, pull the threads through to the wrong side, and tie them.

Smocking. Trimstitch smocking, as shown in Fig. 58, is practical for dress yokes, for sleeves, for holding skirt fullness, for smocks, and for very nice dresses of sheer material. It is especially appropriate for little tots' dresses, and is dainty, yet durable, as it holds securely, the threads in themselves having sufficient strength. The work actually can be done in one-eighth the time that it takes to do hand smocking.

Adjust the stitch to make seven or eight stitches to the inch, and have an ordinary tension. Group your colors as you would for hand smocking and stitch the rows true, so that when shirred up they will be perfectly even. When all the rows are in, stitch across one end of the rows to hold them securely; then, from the opposite end, shirr the stitching up, pulling the bobbin threads only and drawing them all up at the same time. Adjust the gathers evenly, and tie the thread ends; or stitch across them if they terminate in a seam.

Puckering Foot Smocking. Another attractive way to do smocking with Trimstitch is shown in Fig. 59, by stitching diamond or square designs; then make rows of stitching in band effect above and below this, using the sewing machine Puckering Foot.

Couch stitching. Another form of decorative stitching is shown in Fig. 60. This is made by using a heavy thread on the bobbin; and a sewing thread on top. In such cases, the stitching is done from the wrong side, thereby decorating the right side with the bobbin thread. Fig. 61 shows an interesting grouping of couch stitching. Many examples of this form are given elsewhere in this book.

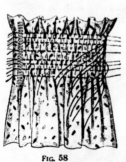

FIG. 58

Decorative stitching by sewing machine makes possible interesting color combinations and decorates and finishes at the same time—all at a minimum of time and effort.

FIG. 59

FIG. 60

FIG. 61

Time Saving Helps

IN SEWING for children keep on hand a generous supply of bindings, tapes, elastics, buttons, notions, and other accessories that are frequently needed. Buy the same kind of buttons for all garments so that if a button is lost it can easily be replaced. Plan to make hems the same width in all garments that need elastic; then buy elastic by the bolt in a width suitable for the hems. In this way new elastic can be put in when needed without inconvenience. Make hems a scant ¼ inch wider than the elastic. ⁵⁄₁₆-inch elastic is satisfactory in ½-inch hems.

When you alter a pattern before cutting or in fitting, make the alterations permanently in the pattern so that you can cut other garments by the corrected pattern. Several garments cut at one time means a saving of time in cutting and in finishing, and invariably allows you to use your materials to better advantage. In cutting, take the precaution to press materials first so that the pattern may be laid on smoothly.

If picoted ruffles are used, mark them so that you can cut through the center of each picoted section and thereby have two widths of ruffles without waste of hemstitching.

Always clip and press seams open inside hems and under facings. This will give a more flat effect and make ironing easier. Be sure also to trim away bulky seams under facings and before applying bindings. This saves time and makes for greater perfection in working.

When sewing buttons on, always place pins crosswise on top of the button and under the thread (see Fig. 63). This uses up more thread and as a result the button lifts up far enough from the garment to

FIG. 62

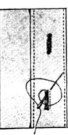

FIG. 64

allow space for the buttonhole to fit under. Use a double thread heavier that your stitching thread in sewing buttons on and in making buttonholes. Bring the thread through to the wrong side under the button and take a few secure whipping stitches over the first threads to hold the button securely. In making buttonholes, outline the buttonholes before cutting, with machine stitching, as in Fig. 64. The stitching makes a firmer buttonhole and insures a straighter edge. Take buttonhole stitches close together, make the purl even and your stitches shallow enough to be attractive. Work a small buttonhole bar across each end.

Use your sewing machine attachments wherever possible, for ruffling, hemming, binding, tucking, quilting. They will save time and perfect your work, and they will give you in the end smartness and serviceability. Making clothes for children is simple when the attachments are put into use.

FIG. 63

School Clothes

FIG. 65 FIG. 66

THERE are a few times in the year when a new dress seems a necessity. The first day of school is one. Children bounce off to school with alacrity when their clothes are new and in keeping with the occasion. Mothers too are filled with satisfaction and pride in knowing that their little folks are correctly attired.

Six school dresses and six pairs of bloomers are none too many for a little girl to begin a school year with. Every child at school or home should be clean and look well put together in her clothes. Stringy belts, dangling sleeves and skimpy skirts are not for school wear. In selecting designs remember these points and choose those that have enough fullness in the skirt to allow the child to move about and sit comfortably and gracefully. In every possible case make bloomers to match the dress, using either the same material or material of the same color in lighter weight.

Good taste, another asset that mothers can help cultivate, means first, all avoidance of anything showy or over done. Simplicity is the one measure by which school clothes must be made. Buy fabrics for school with regard, first, to becomingness of color and texture to the child. Then consider the fabric as to its practicability and ease in laundering. Next choose designs that will be flattering, yet comfortable.

Buster Brown collars are simple, yet lovely for slender faced girls. For those of round face V or square necks look best. Girls of either broad or slender hips generally look better in one piece dresses than in two piece or those with definite waist lines.

In every case, dresses should be planned to be just the right length, just the right size around the waist, and never too big or too little. Correct size for children is very important, if they are to feel well dressed. Wrist bands should be arranged to open so that the hands may be washed as often as is necessary with comfort.

It is a good idea when white or light colored collars and cuffs are used, as in Fig. 66, to bind the lower edges with the dress fabric. This proves a real protection and the soil does not show too quickly.

Bands for the tops of bloomers that button to an underwaist at the center front and back only are usually more certain to stay to place than elastic. This is especially true for active children.

Snap fasteners, if three or five are used, are satisfactory, but when more fasteners are necessary, buttons are better. Loops of narrow woven tape stitched in with the neck and sleeve facings, make good fasteners for small buttons and are quicker to make than buttonholes.

26

Play clothes should be provided so that the school clothes may be taken off and kept in good condition. Mothers can protect themselves and their children by making a plan and interesting their children in adhering to it; that is, to have certain outfits for school and others for play, that they may always be dressed correctly for both.

First School Dresses. Types of dresses especially appropriate for kindergarten and for girls up to eight or ten years of age are shown in Figs. 65 and 66. Their charm is in their simplicity, their value in their practical becomingness and ease of upkeep.

The waist line frock, Fig. 65, is one that is ever popular. Fashion varies the position of the waist-line and the depth of the skirt. Sometimes the skirt comes up under the arms. Sometimes it is half and half, as in Fig. 65. Again, the waist part is two-thirds the length of the dress, as in Fig. 67. Occasionally fashion makes the waist three times as long as the skirt, the skirt serving simply as a deep ruffle. In such cases, the waist usually takes on a slight flare to provide the right fulness through the hips.

In trimming a frock with white, such as shown, buy the white material of the same quality as the dress material, or use organdie, lawn,

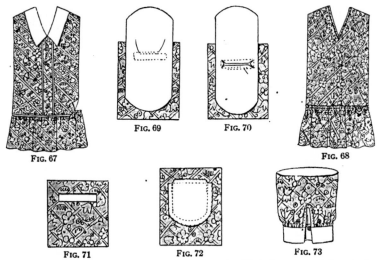

FIG. 69

FIG. 70

FIG. 67

FIG. 68

FIG. 71

FIG. 72

FIG. 73

FIG. 67. Seam the skirt, put the hem in, shirr the waist-line, seam the waist, and place the center front band with its applied edge; then pipe the waist-line as shown.

FIG. 68. The center front band is applied, not inserted. Put the collar on with a bias facing, mitering it at the center front.

FIG. 69. Place the welt stand pocket piece over the pocket location right side of garment. Stitch in the center of the piece. The second double stitch row comes ¾ inch above.

FIG. 70. Slash the opening, fork the corners to the stitching line as shown, and turn back the pieces to the wrong side. Bring the welt piece up on the right side.

FIG. 71. Work the corners of the welt piece out so that the stand fills the space exactly. Lift the lower pouch piece up and stitch the pocket slash seam to the stand, thus holding it permanently to place.

FIG. 72. Stitch around the pouch, staying the corners by stitching them twice. Overcast the edges with close stitches. Press back from the right side.

FIG. 73. Bind the sleeve opening, gather the fulness, and stitch and turn the folded cuff band before applying it. A tape loop is used for the fastening.

27

fine linen, or piqué. Muslin rarely makes appropriate trimming for fine gingham or print frocks. The texture should be in harmony always. In buying designed fabrics, it is often well to buy ½ to 1 yard of the same fabric in plain white or in one of the colors in the fabric, to be used as trimming. Thus there can be no possibility of erring in the texture.

Fig. 66 is the same type of frock as those on page 22. The tab front, which is bound and slipped through the bound slots, gives it a dignity appropriate for school. If desired, a buttonhole may be worked in the tab and this buttoned down to the dress, thus making it possible to open it out for ironing. The binding is of the dress material, the bloomers cut as in *b*, page 22. Fig. 77 has a stand-up collar and turn-back cuffs.

Variations of Slips. When dresses of flimsy or sheer material are worn, .even with bloomers, slips become necessary. When slips are worn the bloomers and the slip should be of the same color. Three simple slips are illustrated here, each having points that make it suited to special dresses. They should be made the same back and front, as they slip readily over the head and require no openings.

FIG. 74

FIG. 75

FIG. 78

FIG. 74. Make center front tab separate; then tack it under the collar, using loop tape for fastening. Button under the collar

FIG. 75. Bind neck slash before collar or tab is applied. Also make bound slash buttonholes.

FIG. 76

FIG. 76. Join bias binding, and stitch it on, raw edges turned in. Make the second stitching on right side, just outside the binding. catching the under binding only.

FIG. 79

FIG. 78. Front trimming piece serves as a facing for the neck opening. Stitch the collar to the band, seam edges inside. Place loops and buttons opposite to hold closing neatly.

FIG. 79. Stitch trimming piece right side to wrong side of pocket, bring it to right side, and stitch it down; then stitch the pocket to place.

Fig. 80 is appropriate for wear under a sheer pinafore "pantie" frock, especially one of delicate color. To make this slip, French seam the shoulder and under-arm seams, bind the neck, armholes and bottom edge, using the fabric of the slip or ready made binding. A point to remember in binding scallops with the machine binder is to avoid making the scallops too deep or pointed. In using the binder bring the point between the scallops straight in line with the binding so that it will be caught the full seam depth and therefore stay securely inside.

The slip in Fig. 81 is a little more ornate. Because of the slash at the waist-line it is more suitable for a dress with a waist-line effect. Should you desire to finish this slip more simply than is shown, you may have a scalloped lower edge and bound neck and armhole edges, the same as in Fig. 80. In the illustration the neck and armhole edges are hemmed and narrow lace is applied. The slash across the hip-line with its gathers gives a straight under-arm seam and provides desirable fulness for the skirt at the same time. In this case the lower edge of the slip has lace trimming with machine made tucks above it.

If a more sturdy slip is desired, tucks and a hem may finish the lower edge, or tucks and a narrow ruffle, or just a plain hem. A scalloped edge is desirable when the slip is to be worn with dresses of varying length.

A tailored type of slip, such as Fig. 82, is very practical. Inverted plaits at the hips provide needed fulness. The straightness of the slip insures ease in making and ironing. Such a slip requires no pattern. Simply measure from under the arm to the knee, or to a point which accords with the length of the dresses worn. Cut the slip this length plus the top and bottom seam allowances. Measure the figure around the hip bones and cut the slip 8½ inches larger than this measurement—8 inches for the plaits and ½ inch for seams.

There need be but one full length seam—that coming on the left side. The other seam can extend from the top down to the plaits only. The material that is cut away above the plaits may be used for the straps. A pressed open, overcast seam is best for the under-arm since so much of it comes inside the hem. A shallow seam that tapers to a point inside of the plait is used in stitching the plait to place. The raw edges of the seams are overcast.

FIG. 80

FIG. 81. In buying lace or embroidery yardage to trim such a slip, choose a fine, closely woven type. Large open hole lace is rarely appropriate and invariably catches and tears.

FIG. 81

FIG. 82. The shoulder straps may be stitched in as the top hem is put in, then the top of the hem caught to the strap from the wrong side, which will hold it in place.

FIG. 82

Combination Suits

FIG. 83

WHEN white or light colored dresses are worn, or dark colored dresses whose color might rub off, or when wool or a coarse fabric makes the bloomers that might scratch, combination suits are worn underneath.

For light colored dresses they may be made of the same fabric as the dress, or of nainsook or gingham of the same color.

The two most generally preferred types of combination suits are shown here. Fig. 83 has a shaped crotch that allows a very plain garment without bulk around the waist. The neck and sleeve edges are hemmed. The lower edge is finished with an elastic. The back closing is made as in Fig. 85. The placket opening is bound with a lengthwise piece cut 2 inches wide, making it ¾ inch wide when folded and seamed to place. Sturdy buttons and buttonholes fasten the center back and hold the back waist-line together.

The pantie combination, Fig. 84, has a bound buttonhole strip made according to instructions in "Short Cuts to Home Sewing", page 28. The neck, armholes and lower edge have a hem made with the foot hemmer, with lace sewed on at the same time that the hem is stitched. The back closing is the same as for Fig. 83, except that the hem across the back waist is omitted. The lower edge is hemmed with the foot hemmer and a piece of tape or lengthwise strip of material ½ inch wide is stitched on from the wrong side at a point in line with the waist-line, to give support to the buttons. Such a garment may be made with the waist and panties in two pieces, or it may be made all in one with the back opening as just described.

The precautions necessary in making such garments are that they should have enough fulness and length in the crotch, that the neck should be cut low enough so that it will not show above the slip or dress, and that the armhole should be large enough that it will not crowd the armhole of the dress.

FIG. 84

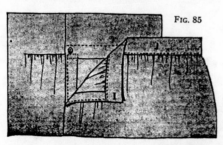

FIG. 85

Night Clothes

FASHION books invariably give a variety of attractive, simple designs for night clothes from which to choose. Fig. 86 can be worn by both boys and girls of one to eight years. After eight years the pajama suit Fig. 89 is more to the liking of children. The night dress in Fig. 87 is a type in favor from the layette days. Design 88, known as a kimono night dress, is especially cool and dainty for a little girl.

The fabrics suited for night clothes are various qualities of soft muslin, double fleeced cotton, known as flannelette, crinkled crepe, cotton crepe, linen, broadcloth, suiting, and closely woven silks. Usually machine stitching serves as the only trimming for such garments.

To make Fig. 86, French seam the shoulder, under-arm, and sleeve seams. Apply the Buster Brown collar with a bias facing. Stitch the armhole seams for overcasting or for two stitchings rather than for binding or French seams, owing to the thickness of material usually employed. The back waist may have a skirt piece, as in Fig. 84, or it may be finished with a hem across, as in Fig. 85. Use two good-sized flat buttons for the back and three for the waist-line.

French seams are used in stitching Fig. 87. Apply the front band as in Fig. 62, page 25. Apply the collar with a bias facing. Buttons and buttonholes complete the front closing. For very small children the collar is sometimes omitted and the neck and front opening bound, using a tape or ribbon for the neck closing.

In making the pajama suit shown in Fig. 89, put a 1¼-inch hem in the legs, seam them up, and join the crotch seam from the back waist-line around to the front waist-line. For boys leave a 2-inch hem opening in the front 4 to 6 inches above the crotch. Put a hem in the top for a tie tape; work buttonholes 2 inches each side of the front seam on the right side, cutting the buttonholes through the top part of the hem only.

French seam the body of the coat and sleeves and hem the sleeve edges and bottom of the coat. Join the sleeves with a plain, overcast seam, bind the neck opening, and apply the double bound edge collar with a bias facing. A loop and button close the front neck.

French seam the night dress in Fig. 88, hem the bottom, gather the neck, and apply the binding to neck and sleeve edges.

FIG. 86   FIG. 87   FIG. 88   FIG. 89

Apron Frocks

ONE of the best garments on which to teach sewing to little girls is an apron frock, such as illustrated in Fig. 90. Apron frocks are usually made for home wear and if an error is made in construction or the finishing is not quite so perfect as mother would make it, it is not so serious as in a dress for school wear. Worn school dresses may have the trimming removed and neck and sleeves bound, thus making apron frocks for house wear.

The neck of the dress must be cut to measure 2 inches more than the head plus the depth of the back slash, so that the dress will slip on and off easily. Bias bindings should be cut from pieces of the material to bind the back neck slash and to face the neck and sleeves. The collar and cuff pieces should be placed right sides of each section together, and then stitched and turned. Machine stitching is added ¼ to ⅜ inch from the edge. The collar and cuffs should be pinned to place on the dress, a bias facing piece pinned on, and then stitched to position. A tape loop should be placed at the right side of the neck opening under the facing for the button that is sewed to the left side.

The pockets should be made and stitched on, then the hem put in, tie sash stitched and turned, the ends stitched across, and tiny straps of the material made and stitched to the side seams at the belt line to hold the sash to place.

The apron rompers (Fig. 91) used by gymnasium classes, girls in rehearsal and for little girls' play suits, represent in construction the same principles as Fig. 90 for the upper part, and Fig. C, page 22, for the lower part. Such a garment may be made of any firm cotton fabric. Shoulders may be cut kimono style, or set in sleeves used. Neck and sleeves may be bound or faced with contrasting color. Wide belt or tie sash may be used, also pockets.

Because one needs to get into the garment through the neck, a back slash is necessary even though the neck measures enough to put the garment on over the head.

FIG. 92. A square of material measuring 28 to 30 inches makes an attractive apron. The edges are machine hemmed, also the strings and neck band. One corner is turned down for a bib. Neck band is sewed on, then the strings placed asshown.

For a more ornate apron, binding or rick-rack may be used for the edges. Pockets may be placed on each side of the center front.

FIG. 92

FIG. 91

Mending Children's Clothes

THE wearing time for clothes, especially wash garments, can be greatly prolonged by mending them when mending proves a protection. Fabrics that have worn thin in spots can often be re-enforced by fine sewing thread used on the machine. In doing this use a medium stitch and stitch back and forth over the thin place to strengthen the worn part. Where necessary, to give additional strength, put a piece of lawn or net underneath the thin place and then darn it by machine.

When a patch is applied, match the warp and woof threads as well as the fabric design. If a new piece of material must be added to a worn garment that has lost color and firmness, wash the new piece several times that it will more nearly agree with the material of the garment. In applying patches by machine, turn the edges, clip the seam allowance at the corners, and press the patch; then pin it to place on the garment. Stitch exactly on the edge, pivoting your needle at each corner so that the patch will appear neat. Cut the material away under the patch and overcast the raw seams, or stitch them from the wrong side to make the edges secure. In patching heavy material, such as khaki, cut out the worn part, place the patch underneath, turn the raw edges around the hole in, and stitch or whip them down.

In mending wool, pull a thread from a lengthwise edge of the fabric and use this thread to darn the worn place. Darning cotton of the right color may be blended in with the lengthwise fabric threads so that the mending stitches will not show.

Long union suits can have the sleeves cut off above the elbows, the legs above the knees, and the worn places thus cut away. When the edges are hemmed, such suits become whole again and are desirable for wear through the spring.

Boys' blouses that have grown shabby around the collars and cuffs may be cut down to a semi-low neck and short sleeves, making comfortable play shirts for warm weather. Little girls' school dresses make admirable play dresses for summer by the same plan.

In lengthening dresses, insert one or two bands above the hem. Cut this band on the bias if the material is a plaid or check, or on the length if it is a stripe, or use a plain fabric if the dress is a print. In making garments that will later need lengthening, use hems one-third deeper than usual. When necessary, open the hem and make a new hem, folding the material so that the stitching line of the new hem comes exactly on the line that marked the bottom of the first hem. The stitching thus conceals the crease line and strengthens it if it is worn.

A deeper band cuff may be added to sleeves, or the cuff may be removed and a band inserted. If a dress needs lengthening and there is not enough material or trimming to insert a band in the skirt, a band may be put in above the belt line about ¼ of the waist length, and a corresponding one put in the sleeves if necessary.

In rejuvenating garments, work to retain a correct balance in design, to equalize the wearing quality, and to harmonize colors so that alterations and adjustments will be blended inconspicuously.

Occasion Frocks

WHEN an occasion frock is needed, or a special dress-up dress is desired, what to choose that will not seem too ornate or elaborate for a little girl is a problem. As a general rule the fabric alone will help to make the difference between a play or school frock and one for the birthday party, for Sunday School wear, or for best dress-up.

Make it a point in planning such a dress to see the dresses in smart shops, in fashion books, and on well dressed children. In this way you can often discover just the dress that will be right for your little girl. Seeing smart dresses will also help in keeping the dress simple, which is important even for dress-up frocks.

FIG. 93

Charming cottons of novelty weave and designed silks, linens and rayons are often used for such dresses. Each year lace, embroidery, ribbon or contrasting fabric in some form serves as trimming to give them fashion value. Therefore consider carefully. Do not use Irish lace when organdie is the vogue. Adapt your trimming to the mode.

In occasion frocks some form of sleeve is usually made—either a puff sleeve, as in Fig. 93, or a ruffle, or an extension band that gives a suggestion of a sleeve. Skirts should be full or should have a lower edge trimming to make them important. When trimming is used at the top of a dress, it should be omitted at the bottom, and vice versa. Shirrings, bindings and facings should be as dainty as possible. Heavy bindings and trimmings do not belong on children's clothes, and especially not on their dress-up dresses.

The dress illustrated in Fig. 93 is typical of a semi-formal frock appropriate for wear by girls four to ten years. The dress itself is of fine dotted swiss. The organdie ruffles and bindings match in color the dot in the fabric.

In making this dress, French seam the raglan shoulders and add the shirrings to the neck and sleeves. Use a narrow double binding for the neck and for the back slash, as in Fig. 94, as well as for the bottom of the sleeves. To make a double binding, cut your bias piece as usual. Fold it through the center and stitch the raw edges to the raw edge of the dress. Bring the folded edge over and stitch or whip it down. If it is to be stitched down, stitch the raw edges to the wrong side of the dress. If it is to be whipped down, stitch the raw edges to the right side of the dress. In this case the binding is whipped down and a small hook and eye used to fasten the dress at the neck.

Organdie, fine voile, lawn and batiste stretch irregularly when cut on the bias. Fabrics of coarser texture are best on the bias, and for bias ruffles of the width and kind shown in Fig. 93, cut the ruffles ¼ to ½ inch wider than the desired finished width because bias ruffles have a

34

tendency to shorten in making. In making organdie ruffles as shown, mark the organdie crosswise. Cut them for hemming or mark for hemstitching, as in Fig. 95. For this measure the distance of the ruffle plus the heading and run a basting thread straight across on the thread, making as many rows of basting as you require widths of ruffles. If no heading is to be used for the hemstitched ruffles, place the basting the width of two ruffles apart so that you can cut through the center of the hemstitching and have two ruffling pieces for each line of hemstitching.

After the dress has been seamed up and the length determined, mark the location of the ruffles. The lower edge of the dress should follow the outline decided on for the ruffles and should be hemmed or picoted to correspond with them. In shaping for scallops it is a good idea to fold the dress and measure its half width; then with a piece of newspaper of this width make an even number of scallops. Shape the scallops attractively, curving them rather slightly, as the ruffles look best when a scalloped line is not too pronounced. After the scallops are shaped, move the paper until a scallop comes across the center front. Never begin or end a scallop at the center front or back. Pin the paper to place on the dress and mark the line with a tracing wheel, pencil, chalk or pins. Pin the gathered ruffles to place, taking care to space them evenly and adjust the fullness attractively. Complete the ruffled joinings with a neat seam and stitch the ruffles to place, stitching directly on top of the gathering thread.

Avoid clumsy seams and joinings on dainty frocks. The art of fine French finishing is to have small bindings, hems and edges, and to eliminate all possible bulk inside hems and joinings. Your sewing machine makes a sturdy, secure seam. You can trim away thicknesses fairly close to the seam. In doing this, if the material frays easily; stitch the seam twice to prevent its pulling away.

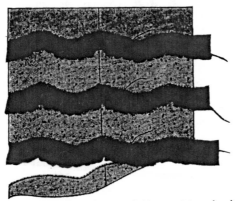

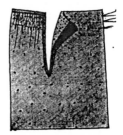

FIG. 94. In drawing up the shirrings to fit around the neck, it is best to put the garment on and draw the shirrings so that they fit exactly, first pinning the neck together at the back.

FIG. 95. In cutting hemstitching apart to make picoted edges, hold the hemstitching line straight ahead and cut accurately so as not to clip the picoted line. Adjust the fulness of the ruffles evenly   Materials for shirring usually require 1½ times to double the length of the place that they are to occupy. For example if the skirt measures 1½ yards around, each ruffle will take 2¼ yards if 1½ times the width is used, or 3 yards if double the width is used. Adjust your gatherer correctly, then your ruffle will fit to space perfectly.

Clothes for Boys

Boys' clothing, like clothing for men, falls into types more easily than that for the feminine world.

Boys' clothes made of ordinary material and ordinarily made are not an economy whether made at home or purchased ready made. If ordinary clothes satisfy, it is better to buy them ready-made than to take the time to make them. When good quality material, good workmanship, and appropriate colorings and fabrics are combined, there is distinct economy in making garments for small boys at home, because these elements are to be found only in the best quality ready-made garments.

Styling clothes for boys is just as important as for girls. Garments must be selected rightly as to fabric and color and must be well cut, thoroughly sewed, and appropriate for their purpose. In choosing fabrics one might for a wee little fellow, perhaps two years old, use a voile blouse and handkerchief linen trousers, but for a four-year-old, one would use handkerchief linen for the blouse and round thread linen for the trousers, while for an eight-year-old, a broadcloth blouse and heavier linen trousers would be more appropriate.

FIG. 96

Suits 96–A and 96–B are cut from the same pattern. A, being tailored severely, would be best for a three-year-old, while B would be more appropriate for a two-year-old because it is daintier in finish. Little boys from two years up can wear suit C, while the overcoat at D is suitable for boys from one year to ten or twelve. As the boy grows older, however, the flare at the lower edge decreases.

The suit shown in Fig. 96 may be worn by small and junior boys. Boys older than eight would have the buttons omitted and hold the trousers and blouse together with a belt, as in Fig. 97, or the trousers would be shaped to fit the hips and no belt worn.

The blouse shown in Fig. 96 is known as a "four-in-hand" blouse, or junior shirt. In Fig. 98 a double-breasted blouse is seen, and in Fig. 97 a sport shirt. These three types are the favored types of boys' blouses and are masculine enough to have their own appeal.

In making garments for boys it is a good idea to keep at hand garments similar to the ones you are sewing which fit correctly. Few little fellows relish interruptions, especially for fitting, so it is best to take measurements and use garments as a guide for measuring sleeve lengths, collar and cuff sizes, pocket positions, and so on. Check your patterns in each part. A collar that is too wide, a cuff that is too heavy, or a yoke that dominates the blouse, destroys proportion and takes away from the garment's essential smartness.

Making Blouses. To make the blouse shown in Fig. 96, join the shoulder seams so that they come to the right side. Apply the shoulder yoke and finish the front hems, remembering to arrange the lap opposite to that for a girl's dress; that is, button it from left to right rather than from right to left. In this case the collar and cuffs are cut on the fold of the material. The inside edge of the collar is shaped slightly to fit the neck of the blouse. The cuffs are straight. Two buttons are sewed together and four buttonholes worked, the buttons serving as cuff links. A little straight four-in-hand tie, a straight back yoke, and a welt pocket have their part in making the whole effect of this garment attractive.

Put the welt pocket in; then stitch the sleeves in, using a flat fell seam, the overlapped seam extending from the blouse rather than from the sleeve. Put the final stitching in from the right side. Stitch the under-arm and sleeve seams, with the back of the blouse and sleeves overlapping the front.

Hem or bind with a lengthwise piece the tiny slashes for the cuff openings. Sew the ends of the cuffs together and stitch them to place on the garment. Stitch the ends of the collar and apply it, concealing all seams by felling the free edge down over the seam. Hem the lower edge of the blouse and seam up and turn the four-in-hand tie. Work a buttonhole loop or sew a fine tape underneath the collar in the back to hold the tie to position. Work the buttonholes in the blouse and sew a tiny piece of fabric to the wrong side of the blouse exactly under the spot where each of the waist-line buttons comes. This will give strength and prevent the buttons from tearing the fabric.

To make the sport shirt shown in Fig. 97, flat fell the shoulder seams. Turn the front facings back and pin them to place. Seam the collar ends, turn the collar right side out, and apply it to the blouse, the underneath collar stitched to the right side of the shirt. Stitch the top edge of the collar to the facing piece. Press the seam open inside the facing and fell the collar down across the back. Stitch $\frac{1}{2}$ inch inside the edge from the bottom of the blouse up and out to the edge of the collar, then around the collar and down the other side.

Put the hems in the top of the patch pockets. Turn the raw edges in and stitch the pockets to place. Join the sleeves with a flat fell seam. Apply the cuffs. Flat fell the under-arm and sleeve seams, stitch the lower edge, and complete the blouse by sewing the buttons on and working the buttonholes. As will be seen, these come inside the front stitching line and serve to hold the facing to place.

FIG. 96–A   FIG. 96–B   FIG. 96–C   FIG. 96–D

37

FIG. 97

To make the double-breasted blouse shown in Fig. 98, stitch the shoulder seams to the right side and apply the yoke, stitching the yoke twice at top and bottom, as shown in Fig. 100. Apply the front facings, seaming them from the notch indicating where the collar begins to the waist-line. Stitch the collar, turn it right side out, and join it to the neck, either by a facing or by inserting the edge of the blouse inside of the collar piece and felling the top edge down.

Stitch the sleeves in, using a flat fell seam. Join the cuffs, as in Fig. 100. Stitch the under-arms sleeve seams and hem the bottom of the blouse. Sew the buttons to a stay strip or sew a tiny piece of material underneath each button.

Making Trousers. Trousers that button on to a blouse, as in Fig. 96, are known as "Oliver Twists" or "button-ons." Those in Fig. 97 are called "shorts." Those in Fig. 98 are usually termed "suit trousers" because such trousers are invariably made of wool material and are lined with a closely woven material to prevent scratching. The shape of the legs and the waist-line finish mark the difference between the "button-ons" and the "shorts." The latter have a belt and more flare in the legs.

Fig. 99 shows the construction of a simple, unlined pair of trousers. The center front and center back seams are French seamed. The crotch is seamed with a flat fell seam and the side stitching is done as for a double-stitched welt seam, as in Fig. 99. The lengthwise buttonholes are placed on the hemmed or faced top in Fig. 96. If a belt is used, as in Fig. 97, belt straps are sewed on the right side in the same location as the buttonholes.

To make the trousers shown in Fig. 98, seam the trousers up and press all seams open. Stitch the darts in the back and then seam the lining exactly the same as the outside. Seam the legs of the lining and the trousers together and press the seams open. Clip the seams at any point where they might draw. When the lining is pulled back in place all seams will be concealed.

Turn the cloth edges in at the side placket openings and fell the lining down over them. Open the center front seam of the outside and lining at the necessary point in the front. Sew a small lined flap to the right front and fell the lining down over the seam of the left front. Whip the ends of this opening securely so that they will not tear out.

FIG. 98

Turn the lining in at the top and stitch or fell it down. If a belt is used, stitch through the trousers and lining the width of the belt from the top to hold the lining to place. If the trousers are made for a small boy, sew a buttonhole band to the inside so that the trousers may be buttoned to the blouse. (Buttonhole banding may be bought by the yard.) Stitch the band in, stitching through the band, lining and trousers. Bind the cut ends of the buttonhole band and tack the band to the lining half way between each two buttonholes. Complete the trousers by sewing buttons at the waist line at the top of the back placket openings.

Novelty belts and mannish buckles may be bought at reasonable prices. These add smartness to a suit and give pleasure to a boy. Metal buckles are usually better than pearl buckles on boys' suits and 4-hole buttons better than 2-hole buttons.

If pockets are desired in trousers, make a lengthwise pouch twice as long as the side opening and 3 to 4 inches wide. Pin these pouch pieces at one side. Sew one side of the opening to the front placket opening. Face the other side with the material of the trousers, doing this so that the lining piece that is used for the pocket will not show from the side. Catch the top of the pocket in with the waist line finish. Stitch across the bottom of the pouch and overcast the seam. Welt pockets are occasionally put in the hips of boys' trousers. These are made exactly the same as the welt pocket described on page 27, except that the welt is narrower.

When trousers are finished, press them through the center of the legs, just as men's trousers are pressed, creasing them carefully. Always press wash trousers in the same way. Boys' bloomers, which are made the same as trousers except that they are cut longer and have a band to hold them in at the knee with a buckle at the side, are pressed so that the creases come at the sides rather than at the center front and back of the legs.

Styling Clothes for Boys. In choosing colors and materials for boys' clothes, see the best quality garments. Find the colors and types that you know will be appropriate for the child for whom you are planning the clothes, so that you will be sure to have the right style effect.

Avoid by all means using feminine fabrics in boys' attire. The point is to have them just as smartly masculine as possible, even when boys are tiny. The yardage for such garments is small and one can afford to buy materials that are right for the purpose. A wise mother will see the advantage of making herself proficient enough in sewing so that she can make trousers and blouses look like custom-made garments. The sewing machine and the iron are the two greatest aids to smart, tailored effects.

In Fig. 100, as shown, double stitched edges and flat fell seams appear much the same.

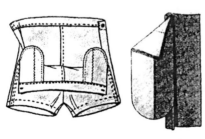
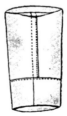
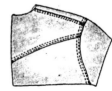

FIG. 99   FIG 99A   FIG. 100

Middies and Bloomers

MIDDY and bloomer suits suitable for play, and especially suitable for camp wear, appeal to girls from six years up. The illustration shown in Fig. 101 is an approved type of simple, short-sleeved middy and half plaited, elastic knee bloomers.

A sport suit such as this should be of firm material. that will hold its shape and be appropriate for the purpose for which it is made. Any firm, closely woven cotton suiting, khaki, or serge fabric is suitable. The middy may be of a lighter color than the bloomers; for instance, the bloomers may be of khaki color, which is an olive drab, and the middy of a harmonizing tan or white. Again, the suit may be made all of blue in one tone, or midnight blue serge may be used for the bloomers, and middy blue for the middy. The regulation gymnasium suit shown in Fig. 110 has white twill middy with navy serge bloomers. This type of suit is necessary for gymnasium work, and is generally approved for school sports for girls.

The points to remember in making these sturdy garments are: to use coarse thread, to stitch all seams securely, and to stitch back on all seams to make them durable. Such garments should have a tailored air, which is achieved by the appropriate selection of material, the simplicity of the design, and the prominence of the stitching.

Making Bloomers. To make the bloomers as shown in Fig. 101, join the front and back sections together, using a flat fell seam. There is no seam at the center front or center back of the bloomers, as they are cut on a fold of the material. When the crotch seam is completed, join the sides in a plain seam if the edges are selvage, and press them open. If the edges are cut, make a double-stitched seam, the same as for the crotch.

Measure around the figure to determine just how long the band should be. Allow 4 inches at each side for overlapping. As the band in this case fits rather closely to the figure, it is better to have it at least 2 to 2½ inches deep. When the two sections of the band, front and back, are ready, pin the center front of the bloomers to the center front band, and then lay the plaits in, adjusting the fulness so that the plaits will be even and extend out to within 3 or 4 inches of the side seams. Stitch bias pieces of the material together, as in Fig. 103, and use them for the loops in the belt, as in Fig. 104. Stitch these loops in place and then bring the belt or band over and stitch it down permanently. These loops, if they are made of the material, should each be 2¾ inches long and 1 inch wide when cut. Turn the raw edges in ¼ inch and stitch the strip to hold the turned in edges. In placing the loops in position the stitching line comes inside of each loop.

Put the hem in the bottom of the bloomers for the elastic, and sew two buttons to each side for closing, placing pins across the top of the button under the thread, as instructed on page 25.

For the regulation bloomers shown in Fig. 110, the weight of the fabric and the strenuousness of the sports regulate to some extent the method of finishing. Heavy serge has a plain seam stitched with coarse linen thread, the raw edges of the seams bound with bias binding. Light weight serge may have French seams, as in Fig. 105.

Fig. 105 shows how the plaits are laid, how the placket opening is

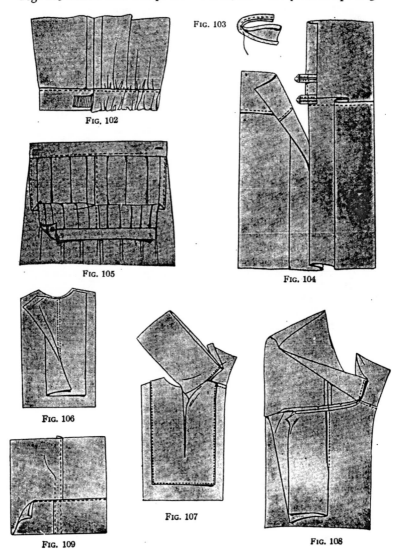

Fig. 103

Fig. 102

Fig. 105

Fig. 104

Fig. 106

Fig. 107

Fig. 109

Fig. 108

bound with a lengthwise strip, and how a narrow lengthwise band is used. This is held together with a buttonhole and button at each side.

Making Middies. To make the middy as shown in Fig. 101, French seam the shoulder seams and hem the bottom of the sleeves, using a plain 1-inch or 1¼-inch hem. Place the front facing piece over the front of the blouse, as in Fig. 106. Place two rows of stitching 1⅛ inch each side of the center front line, tapering the stitching to a point at the bottom. Slash between the two rows of stitching from the neck down to the point, but do not cut into the stitching. Overcast around the point so that it will not fray out, turn the applied piece to the wrong side of the middy, and turn and crease the raw edges in.

Apply the collar piece as in Fig. 107, stitching it first across the back neck and out to the center front seam. Stitch the top of the collar to the facing piece, as in Fig. 108, press the seam open, and clip the edges. When the lower collar has been stitched to the neck, the top collar to the facing piece, as shown, the seam will be entirely concealed by whipping the top collar down over the back neck seam.

Stitch the facing piece down to the blouse, or stitch the creased edges and then tack the facing to place, doing this so that the stitches will not show on the right side.

French fell the under-arm seams, making the stitching as shown in Fig. 109. Turn the hem either to the right or wrong side and stitch it to place. Occasionally loops of the fabric are sewed in the side seams at the bottom hem with buttons back of them. These are used to button the garment in close to the hip line. Sometimes it is the fashion to make the middy longer than those shown here and to use a plain hem at the bottom with a separate belt above.

A bias tie of silk is usually the only decoration for a middy such as shown in Fig. 101. If only one tie is to be made, it is sometimes better to buy it ready made. If two sisters or chums are desirous of having a tie at the same time, ½ yard of material will make two ties, putting a seam at the center back. These can be very easily made by hemming them with the foot hemmer. Usually the pure colors of red or blue are used for the tie. Occasionally orange or black is favored.

To make the regulation middy shown in Fig. 110, which has an applied yoke with a bias seam at the center back, seam the shoulders to the right side and press the seams open. Seam the applied yoke and press the seam open. Stitch the yoke at the neck opening, right side of yoke to wrong side of middy, so that when it is turned to the right side it will serve as a facing. Turn the raw edges of the back and front of the yoke under and stitch twice, as in Fig. 110, the wide side of the presser foot serving as a gauge for the stitching.

Stitch the braid on the collar and cuffs and join them to the middy, as shown in Fig. 111 and Fig. 112. The braider attachment of the sewing machine is a splendid aid in placing braiding. If this is not used, light pencil marks on the garment should be made and these used as a guide in stitching the first row of braid to place, especially at the corner turns. The presser foot will guide the braid after the first row. Avoid piecing braid. Always make sure that there is enough in the piece to stitch a complete row on the collar. Short pieces may be used for the cuffs. If piecing must be done, arrange it to come at a corner turn. Put the pocket in the front of the blouse, seam up the sleeves, bind the opening as in Fig. 112, and put the cuffs on. Seam up the under-arms, put the sleeves in, and apply the lengthwise band at the bottom, as shown in Fig. 113, using two rows of stitching as for the yoke. Such a band should fit the top of the hips almost snug. If a longer, looser middy is desired, a hemmed lower edge, as in Fig. 101, should be used.

Middies that are to receive strenuous wear, such as those worn for basket-ball, often have the yoke cut to extend down under the arms to give re-enforcement there.

Make the eyelets in the front and run a silk lacer through them, tying it at the top of the opening. A gay, hemmed edge tie of a shape decided upon by the class is often worn over this. The braid may be of white or a color. This also is usually decided by the class. Two buttons and buttonholes on each of the cuffs, as in Fig. 112, complete the middy.

Finish the seams of middies and bloomers as neatly as possible, avoiding bulky joinings that might irritate in wearing. As a rule an athletic union suit is all that is worn under such uniforms; therefore, it is necessary to have smooth, well finished seams, hems and edges.

Knitted one-piece bathing suits are often adopted by a class for practice work in the gymnasium, the middy and bloomer suits being used for exhibition work. Knitted suits should be purchased because the fabric frays easily and requires factory-made, ready-made seams.

Fig. 112

Fig. 111

Fig. 113. In making middies of firm material where lengthwise or bias edges join or overlap cross or lengthwise edges, assemble the pieces on a flat surface, your sewing-machine table serving admirably. Smooth each piece perfectly and pin it to position so that there can be no fulling or stretching.

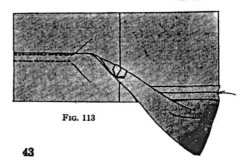

Fig. 113

43

Tailoring for Smartness

Perfect Hems. If you would make perfect hems, observe the following rules:

Turn the hem on the figure, remove the dress, lay it out on the table with the center front and center back lines straight, and even the hem all the way around. Adjust the pins so that the line at the bottom of the skirt is uniform at both sides and that there are no lumps or uneven places anywhere. Measure the depth of the hem, gauging it all from the narrowest place. A cardboard cut just the depth of the hem at its narrowest point is a good guide to use in measuring.

Always take the precaution to press open the seam inside the hem. If the garment is French seamed, simply clip the seam at the top of the hem and pull the first row of stitching out, which will allow the seam to open. Careless sewing is most quickly observed at this point.

There are two ways to finish the top of a slipstitched hem satisfactorily. One is to turn the raw edge under, stitch the turn with the sewing machine, and then use this stitched edge as a foundation for the slip stitches that hold the hem to the dress. The second method, which is preferred for heavier fabrics such as flannels, heavy crepes or satins, is to stitch a seaming ribbon to the top of the hem, then slipstitch the top edge of the seaming ribbon to the dress so that no stitches can show conspicuously on the right side. See illustrations A and C below.

In pressing a hem when it is finished, always place a cloth over the garment on the right side and press from the right side, so that the seaming ribbon or stitched edge will not press through and show.

Before finishing the lower edge of circular skirts, let the skirt hang for forty-eight hours so that it will sag as much as it will. Finish the edge with a facing or binding.

In finishing the edge of plaited skirts, put the hem in before the plaits are made. If any adjustment in length is to be made, do this at the waist line rather than at the bottom.

For hems in circular or flare skirts, as in A, stitch the top of the hem, using a long stitch. Draw up the thread so that the fulness will be evenly distributed. Then baste and slipstitch the hem to place.

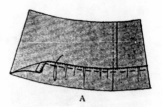

A

When seaming ribbon or bias binding is used at the top of the hem, as at B, place decorative stitching over the ribbon and thus avoid bulk. Press seams open inside hems whenever possible. C shows seaming ribbon stitched on, then slip-stitched to place.

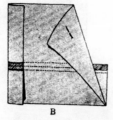

B

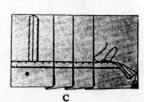

C

44

Clothes for Junior Girls

SCHOOL girls today experience no dreary period of unbecoming clothes between the time they cast off their bloomer frocks and the time they begin to be interested in their own clothing. Girls quickly adapt the new, especially in fashion. If they have been aided in a development of good taste their use of the new will be certain to be complimentary and invariably gratifying as they grow to womanhood.

Schools, and teachers especially, have had a great deal to do with the encouragement of attractive clothing for girls from childhood to young womanhood. Teachers and mothers both are realizing that there need be no awkward age for girls, that if girls' clothing is selected with consideration for appropriateness, individual becomingness, and smartness, a girl can be just as attractive at fourteen as she was at six or will be at twenty. She can be attractive for the age of fourteen.

There is no age at which clothing should not be intelligently discussed with girls, especially after they have reached the age of the fifth or sixth grade. By discussion of clothing and becoming, appropriate attire, good taste and a sense of discrimination are developed that will serve throughout the years.

No mother or teacher should be dictatorial about what a girl should wear. Rather she should encourage the girl to reason and observe and know what is best for herself. Clothing must always be designed to suit the age, temperament and type. Under no circumstances should the clothes of an older person be shortened for a younger one. If the material must be used again, it should preferably be dyed, re-cut and re-made to take on a wholly new life.

Select clothing for school wear with the idea in mind of suitability for the season or climate, means for keeping it clean, and frequency of change.

Plaited skirts, which have been popular for a quarter of a century for school girls, will undoubtedly continue so for a very long period of time, because plaited skirts seem to be absolutely in keeping with the jauntiness that is associated with a girl of school age. This does not necessarily mean an all-around plaited skirt, but plaits to give fulness for walking, and for all the various activities of school life.

The bloused or two-piece type of dress that has enough length in the waist to allow the arms to be lifted without the skirt's hiking up or becoming separated from the waist, is excellent. Sleeves that protect the arms, but that do not get in the way of working, are also an advantage. A natural collar-line that allows the head to bend comfortably for study is important.

Wool, cotton, linen, silk, and rayon can all be used for school frocks. Wool is suitable for general school wear when a school girl is old enough to take care of her clothes.

There was a time when silk was considered in bad taste for school wear, but the tailored silks—flat crepe, crepe de chine, silks that are durable, cleanable and not too expensive—are not inappropriate.

45

Party dresses are never in good taste in the classroom. Dresses of taffeta, or georgette, or lace, are taboo for classroom wear, for the reason chiefly that one cannot possibly keep such dresses clean and fresh and in condition. The expense of taking care of them would be prohibitive to most people, and no matter what the financial circumstances, they should not be worn. In this age of democracy no girl desires to show by her clothes that she is in a better financial condition than her schoolmates. That in itself is considered bad taste. The old adage, "When in Rome do as the Romans do," surely applies to clothes worn by school girls. If all the girls in a class decided to wear cotton frocks, then it would be better for all to go along on that plan and wear cotton frocks, even if an occasional pupil should find it easier or more to her liking to have frocks of silk or wool.

There is a question as to the propriety of silk stockings for classroom wear. Many teachers insist that lisle or light-weight wool stockings are essential for school wear, that silk stockings should not be worn except for parties. With a large group of girls it is usually more economical and practical for the majority to wear lisle stockings than silk ones; therefore, those that can easily afford silk ones should choose to be in harmony with their associates and wear, out of courtesy to them, what they wear. Good quality lisle or wool hose cost as much as do silk hose, but they have the advantage of lasting longer.

No girl should put on a frock at the beginning of the school term and wear it straight through to the holidays without changing. Such a practice is not good for her own morale or for her associates or teacher. If her means are limited, it is better to buy two moderately-priced dresses than one expensive one in order that there may be a change and an opportunity for the dresses to be freshened at intervals.

Girls should learn at the very outset to take care of their own clothing, to remove their school dresses when they come home, and hang them up. They should be taught to freshen their own dresses and press them so they can always look neat and trim and take pride in looking so.

In summing up clothes for school wear, these points should be remembered:

The fabric should be neutral in tone, never delicate in color. It should be becoming above all. It should have an even weave and smooth surface so that it will not catch or pull, and not hold the dirt easily. Flannel or fine serge is preferable to cheviot in this respect, gingham to dotted Swiss, flat crepe to satin, and so on.

Dresses should be cut so that there is ease in the waist-line and sleeves, a becoming line in the collar, and enough fulness in the skirt to allow it to hang gracefully whether the wearer is standing or sitting.

Shoes should never be ornate, but practical and of good material. Hair bows and ornaments should be omitted. A comb or barette, or a ribbon to hold the hair neatly in place, is desirable. Bangles, bracelets, pins, rings and necklaces should not be worn. Bow ties and smart belts are trimming features that are always in good taste. Collars and cuffs of contrasting color are pretty and desirable because they often give freshness to a dress and encourage individual becomingness.

Bloomers are always preferable to petticoats or slips. These should be of a color to harmonize closely with the color of the dress, or match the dress material.

Transparent or elaborately trimmed frocks should never be worn to school. They are quite as undesirable as cosmetics in the classroom. They simply do not belong to the girl who would express good taste, becomingness, and appropriateness in clothes.

A clothes plan is necessary for every girl, no matter whether she goes to school in her home town or city, or to boarding school or college. A certain number of dresses, under-garments, and other clothes for school, sports and athletics are necessary and should be supplied at the beginning of the school year rather than spasmodically and in haste.

Girls going away should send to the school for a list of clothes necessary. When a girl has checked her clothes with the list she will be able to approach the school term without concern as to the completeness or appropriateness of her wardrobe.

For every dress in the wardrobe there should be a place. There should be a coat that will harmonize with the dresses, as well as shoes and a hat. Misfit dresses or hats bought at random without regard to their suitability with other articles of wear are expensive and tragic purchases when expenditures must be considered carefully.

To dress beautifully as a woman, a girl must learn early the value of clothes, their harmony and suitability one garment with another. Then success in clothes will be certain. The art of choosing and wearing clothes is one that cannot be acquired quickly. Cultivation, interest, and a knowledge of what is appropriate are necessary if good taste is to be expressed always.

NOTE: *Patterns for young girls are bought by age, size 6 to 20 and are altered the same as adult patterns. See pages 11-12-13 "How to Make Dresses" Singer Library No. 2.*

Two Piece Frocks

Fig 114

Girls who have grown up quickly and who look overgrown in bloomer dresses and lanky in one piece ones, will welcome the two piece frock The two piece frock and the basque dress are conceded to be the most becoming types to small women and junior girls.

The precautions in making two piece dresses are: to have the waist long enough to cover the skirt and camisole joining, to have the blouse carry an air of comfortable looseness rather than snugness, to select a material that is firm enough in weave to tailor nicely. Cotton crepe, broadcloth, linen, prints, suitings, ginghams, jersey, flannel and tailored silks are suitable.

Tan cotton crepe makes the dress shown in Fig 114. The camisole of the panel plait skirt is also of the crepe, so that there will be no gap if the blouse should slip up. The collar and cuffs are of white crepe of the same texture The decorative stitching is of heavy, fast-color cotton thread, used on top with a coarse needle, with a number 50 or 60 sewing thread used in the bobbin.

Making the Skirt. Simply tear or cut on a thread two widths of material 32 or 36 inches wide, making the lengths measure from the top of the belt to the bottom of the desired skirt length, plus the hem, which in this case is 3½ inches. Where attention is called to a hem by means of decoration, as in Fig. 114, a generous hem is advisable. When a narrow hem is necessary, finish it inconspicuously. When a dress is plain it should look as though you intended it so, not because of lack of material.

Seam the selvage edges of the two widths together. Clip the selvage every few inches to prevent its tightening in washing Turn the hem at the lower edge and baste it to place; then stitch it with one to three rows of decorative stitching. If decorative stitching is not used, stitch the turned edge of the hem and slipstitch it to place.

When the hem is in, fold the skirt, side seams together, and notch the center front and back at the waist line. Measure the body at the top of the skirt, adding two inches for freedom. Measure the top of the folded skirt and calculate how many plaits you can have and how deep they can be. For example, if you are using 32-inch material, two widths will give you 64 inches less 2 inches for seams, deep seams being necessary to insure taking in all of the selvage. If the body measures 28 inches and you allow 2 inches for freedom, this leaves you 32 inches to be divided into plaits—16 inches for the front and 16 for the back. In this way you will have 4 plaits in the center front and 4 in the back, each plait 2 inches deep, or taking up 4 inches of material. When the plaits are placed, put the skirt on an ironing board, plaited section up, and pin the plaits to place at top and bottom, following the warp threads accurately. Press the plaits in, using a damp cloth. Then stitch across the top of the plaits to hold them in.

Shape the camisole top from a plain waist pattern, making a low, round yoke and large armholes, as for a slip. Make French or plain, pressed open seams at the shoulders and under-arms. Hem or face the neck and armhole edges and join the under-waist portion to the skirt. If the bust is larger in proportion than the hips, dart the under-waist at the waist-line before joining it to the skirt. Sometimes when a skirt hikes out in front it is because of a high chest or bust. Darts at the waist-line in the under-waist will help to correct this.

If a band is used at the top of the skirt and buttoned on to the blouse or under-waist, make a hemmed placket at the top of the left side seam.

The side seams are considered as construction seams in the dress, the same as shoulder seams. In a partially plaited skirt, such as Fig. 114 shows, it is important that they come down straight in line with the under-arms of the blouse and be directly under the arms when they are hanging straight down at the sides.

Making the Blouse. For the blouse of Fig. 114, any plain blouse pattern that has appropriate collar and cuffs may be used. The front shoulders may have shirrings or tucks as desired. The shoulder and under-arm seams may be French seamed or pressed open.

Stitch the shoulder seams first, add the front facing piece, stitching it on the right side, slashing between the stitching lines, and staying the point of the slash with overcast stitches, as explained on page 42. When the facing piece is on, join the collar, first slipping the neck of the dress over the head to make sure the V neck is low enough. Remember that the collar will make it a little higher because of the roll effect. Now measure the collar so that in length it will equal exactly the neck opening plus the end seams. Stitch the seams across the end, turn the collar right side out, and stitch the wrong side of the collar to the right side of the dress, keeping the front facing free. Begin at the front facing seam and collar seam and stitch the facing and top of the collar together, as shown in Fig. 115. Press the seams open and fell the collar seam down across the back of the neck.

The facing pieces for the cuff opening are completed the same as for the front. When these are on, and before the under-arm sleeve seams are stitched, apply the decorative stitching to the front of the blouse and to the sleeves. Fig. 115 shows how the decorative machine stitching replaces the basting, and how the basting has been used to outline the exact line for the stitching. The stitching is taken through the facing pieces, holding them in place.

Stitch the under-arms of the blouse, join the cuffs as the collar was joined, stitch the belt band on, using a double crosswise fold of material for this. Place seams in the band at the sides to correspond with the side seams in the blouse. Apply the decorative stitching to the bottom of the band. Com-

FIG. 115

plete the blouse by sewing a small hook and eye, or a tape loop and button, to the neck opening and on the cuffs; then press finally.

Plaited Skirt Frocks

PLAITED skirts are frequently in fashion. Any fabric that tailors nicely, even georgette, may be used. Plaits may be put in at home very satisfactorily. In making them the lines of the plaits should follow the warp threads and the plaits pressed with a damp cloth under the iron so that the steam will shape the plaits and hold the creases.

Instructions are given for making a partially plaited skirt in connection with the two piece dress illustrated in Fig. 114. The dress illustrated in Fig. 116 is plaited all the way around with ½-inch knife plaits. Because of the many plaits, in this case it would be economy of time to send the material to the plaiter's and have the skirt steam plaited.

Knife plaiting is done in widths of ⅛ inch, ¼ inch, ½ inch, and 1 inch, and box plaits of ¾ to 3 inches. The ¼ to ½ inch width is used most. Accordian plaiting is occasionally used for ballet skirts and requires nearly twice as much material as knife plaiting.

Whatever width of knife plaiting you desire, plan your skirt fulness to equal three times the hip measurement. For example, in using 40-inch fabric for a 35-inch hip measurement, you will need approximately 2½ widths, allowing for seams. If the half width is placed between the two full widths you will avoid a seam at the center front.

FIG. 116

To prepare the material for plaiting, tear the widths or pull a thread for cutting so that they will be perfectly straight with the woof threads. Seam the skirt up, leaving the back seam open, and finish the lower edge. Remember, the flatter the hem the straighter will be the plaits. Bulky hems cause the plaiting to swerve out of line. If wool material of medium weight is used, face the lower edge with silk, allowing the silk to extend out as a piping. Frequently ribbon is used on the wrong or right side. Hercules braid, which is a woven braid, is used in the same way as ribbon and is a little more serviceable for wool skirts. Either the ribbon or the braid is stitched so that 1/16 inch shows below the skirt. The free edge is whipped or stitched to the skirt. Often a tiny tuck is made at the bottom ½ inch from the lower edge; then the ½ inch edge is turned in ⅛ inch and the turned portion whipped to the tuck, which gives a hand-finished binding effect without bulky seams.

In sending plaiting out to be done, specify the width you desire for the plaits and whether you want an inverted plait at the center front or

50

a box plait. Fig. 116 shows a box plait center. If you do not specify the kind, the plaiting will generally be done all one way, the plaits running toward the left.

Leave the plaiting in the paper in which it is returned until you are ready to use it. In stitching the back seam up, begin at the bottom so that the bottom line will be exactly even. Before stitching the seam, baste or pin it so that a true, unstretched seam will result.

When the plaited skirt is to be joined to an under-waist, make the under-waist complete and finish the neck and armhole edges. If the under-waist is too large at the waist line, use darts to make it fit. Join the skirt to it, beginning at the center front and pinning around each way; then stitch the joining with a plain seam. Take care that the plaiting folds in easily without stretching or fulling.

When the skirt is seamed to the waist, if the plaiting is the least bit heavy, turn the seam up and add a second row of stitching on the right side exactly at the bottom of the waist.

When plaiting is to be joined to a band, pin it in place just as for an under-waist, taking care, of course, to have each plait perfectly flat and in its pressed position.

Below are shown hem finishes suitable for plaited skirts. As will be seen, the object is to have the hems as flat as possible.

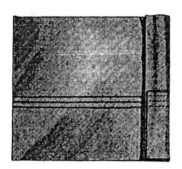

Fig. 117

Fig. 119

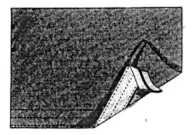

Fig. 118

Fig. 120

51

One Piece Frocks

IN MAKING one piece frocks, take care that the design is not too grown-up in appearance. The collar, cuffs, and skirt fulness are the essential features in the dress shown in Fig. 121. If the collar were ½ inch narrower it would at once appear more mature. If the belt were lower the dress would look as though made for an older person.

In styling such a dress, note the length carefully and see that it is not too long; also that the belt line is not too high or low. Before placing the belt permanently, it is a good idea to pin it to position on the figure and observe it from a distance to make sure that the location is the most becoming possible.

Welt pockets on each side of the center front, placed directly down from the center of the shoulder and 3 or 4 inches above the waist-line, or patch pockets below the waist line, add youthfulness.

In this case, two deep knife plaits are arranged at each side front, the plaits turning back toward the seam. A slash is made under the belt to allow these to be caught to place. The dress has a panel front cut crosswise of the material. The collar and cuffs are double and may be finished with French binding or a narrow piping inserted between the edges of the two thicknesses of collar and cuffs. A short slash is made straight down the center front, the edges finished the same as the collar.

FIG. 121

A tie string or flat tailored bow may be used to finish the collar joining.

The shoulder tucks may be taken from the wrong or right side as desired, or shirrings may be substituted for the tucks.

A slipstitched hem finishes the bottom. The narrow, lengthwise belt is stitched and turned, the slide buckle slipped on, and two fasteners, one on each side, used to hold the slide and belt to place. Belt straps are used at the side seams so that the belt may easily be removed when the dress is laundered.

French Bindings. It is very easy to distinguish between a French-made binding and an ordinary binding. The French bindings are very narrow and neatly done, whereas other bindings are often wide and thick, giving a clumsy appearance to the edge.

To make a French binding, cut a true bias strip from ⅝ to ¾ inch wide, fold it through the center and press it. Stitch the raw edges to the raw edge of the garment, bring the fold over to the wrong side of the garment, and whip it directly over the stitching line. By using a fold in this way and trimming the seam edge close, it is possible to make a secure, flat binding only ⅛ inch wide.

In stitching binding to georgette, lace or chiffon, use paper under the stitching so that neither the binding nor the dress edge will draw. The binding will stretch slightly in handling; therefore, allow it to ease to the edge when it is pinned to place so that it will not appear drawn at any place.

Pipings. In making dresses of sheer material, the edges should be bound as just described. In making dresses of firm fabrics such as satin, heavy cottons and silks, linens, and woolens, in the majority of cases the neck edge should be finished with a piping, or a facing that extends out in piping effect, because such a finish is less bulky in these materials than a binding would be.

If a piping of a contrasting color is used, sometimes it is allowed to extend out 1/16 inch, simply to give a line of color. In every case, on shaped edges, piping should be seamed together and cut on a true bias the same as for a bias binding.

Jaunty Pockets. Jaunty pockets add much to the beauty of tailored garments. Pockets are not difficult to make if one sets about it with a plan. The first thing to do is to determine the correct location of the pocket when the garment is fitted. The perforations on the pattern indicate a general location. It is well to baste a line for this location, and when fitting see if it is the most becoming to the figure. This precaution is taken because it is often necessary to lengthen or shorten a pattern to correspond to the individual height, which naturally changes the location of the pocket. When the position of the pocket has been located, proceed to make the appropriate kind of pocket. (Instructions for making a welt pocket may be found on page 27, patch pockets on pages 22 and 28.)

Smart Buttonholes. In making bound buttonholes, the size, the distance from the edge, and the spacing are the important points. Be sure that the welt edge is true, and take the precaution to baste the welt edges together before pressing the buttonhole. (Instructions for making bound buttonholes may be found on page 15.)

FIG. 122. Place the fulness in the front. Seam the shoulders and finish the neck slash and outside collar edge. Apply the collar with a fitted facing.

FIG. 123. By cutting the cuffs as shown, the edges of the turn back come together, while the underneath part laps over and buttons. By using the trimming for loops and edges the finishing is quickly done.

Fig. 124

Box Plaited Dress. The box-plaited dress shown in Fig. 124 is a type required by many boarding and private schools. Its youthful dignity, plus its simplicity, makes it entirely appropriate for general school wear.

To make such a dress, measure the figure, decide where the plaits should come and what their width is to be. For a child of average proportions they may be a little more than ⅓ of the width of the shoulder and placed nearly in the center. For a narrow shoulder type place the plaits nearer the shoulder and make them slightly wider. For a larger child make the plaits narrower and place them nearer the neck. Measure from the center front line the width and position of the plaits. Baste these accurately in line with the warp threads to a point 1 to 2 inches below the belt line. Flatten the box plaits so that the stitching line will come directly in the center and baste the plaits down, using long diagonal stitches. Press the plaits to a point a few inches below the waist line. A plain dress pattern may be used for cutting box-plaited dresses as the plaits are put in first before the shoulders and neck are cut.

Finish the sleeve seams, using pressed open seams, finish the front and neck opening, and face the neck-line. Set the sleeves in and make the belt and the pocket. Turn the hem and finish it; then finish basting and pressing the plaits to the bottom of the skirt.

Two or three collars should be made for such a dress. The fabric should be linen, piqué or firm wash silk. A wide bias binding should be stitched to the inside edge of the collars, which will finish them, and make it possible to remove the collars for washing.

Tucked Two-Piece Dress. To make the blouse shown in Fig. 125, put the front tucks in. Join the shoulders, then baste the neck band, which is

cut to finish as a facing, to the wrong side, turn it to the right side, turn the raw edge in, and stitch down as shown.

Ribbon or braid may be used for this kind of trimming if less curve is used at the front neck-line, and ribbon seamed at the shoulders and gathered at the top around the curve.

Stitch the side seams, put the waist-line tucks in, making them the same depth and distance apart. Pull the threads through and tie them, finish the sleeves, and finally turn the hem at the lower edge of the blouse. Stitch the edge and then slip-stitch it to place. Belt straps should be used at the side seams to keep the belt centerwise of the waistline tucks.

Fig. 125

Basque Dresses

Dresses having a plain waist and gathered skirt, as in Fig. 65, page 26, are classed as waist-line dresses, and are worn by little girls from three and four up to eight and ten years of age. When the waist portion needs a little shaping at the under-arms, when the skirt takes on more width, and the dresses fit a little closer, as in Fig. 126, then they are called "basque" dresses.

Basque dresses in some form are invariably in fashion, especially for dancing school, confirmation, graduation, and first parties. Such dresses made of attractive cottons are also suitable for girls of school age for summer wear. When they are simply made they are approved by some for school wear.

Plaid material, which might be of gingham, rayon or silk, was used for Fig. 126. The plaid fabric was selected so that the shaping of the lines and the bias skirt, which is frequently used for such dresses, might be better understood.

Dresses of this type may be made entirely by machine, the seaming, shirring and binding all proving more attractive when done by machine than by hand.

A basque dress usually requires slight fulness in the bust. The pattern generally provides for gathers at the front shoulders or gives a gathered dart at the upper front under-arm. The fulness should be so placed as to give an effect of ease to the dress, but not make obvious the effort to provide bust line fulness.

In proportioning such a dress, plan the skirt to measure in width three times that of the waist. For instance, if the waist measure is 28 inches, the skirt should measure approximately 84 inches at the lower edge. The more limp the material, the more skirt fulness there should be. If a designed fabric and bias skirt are used, piece the widths accurately in the skirt so that the design and the warp threads will be brought together correctly and thus make inconspicuous joinings. Fig. 127 shows how the plaids have been brought together and matched regardless of the material. A slight waste of material results in doing this. If the design is large, a greater waste may be experienced, but it is necessary where the right effect is desired.

In making the dress, shirr the top of the skirt with from three to nine rows of group shirring. Draw these shirrings up to fit the waist-line easily. Seam up the blouse portion, either for French seams or for pressed-open, overcast seams. Fit the blouse to the waist-line easy enough so that a side closing will not be necessary; then gather up the shirrings in the skirt to fit the bottom of the waist exactly.

If a corded piping is used at the waist-line, as Fig. 128 shows, cover a small cable cord with a true bias piece, either of the dress material or the trimming material. Baste this cord to the bottom of the waist, and then with your machine cording foot stitch the waist and skirt and corded piping to place. The cording foot will allow the needle to follow very close to the cord and thus wedge it to place.

When the skirt and waist are joined, fit the dress to determine the

FIG. 126

correct length, the becoming neck-line, and the sleeve length. In this case binding that requires two rows of stitching to place it is added to the neck, sleeves and lower edge.

Fig. 129 shows how the scallops are cut to agree with the design in the skirt and how bias binding is stitched first to the right side, then turned and basted to place on the wrong side. A second row of stitching is added to the right side exactly above the binding to catch the binding on the wrong side. This is put in so that when the binding is pressed the right side stitching will not show.

Short, scalloped sleeves and a boat neck are attractive for such a dress. Puff sleeves are also frequently made. Puff sleeves are made by slashing the sleeve pattern and separating it in the center to put in as much as is desired. The sleeve is gathered both at top and bottom and the fulness held in the armhole and in the lower part by a band or bias binding.

A basque skirt such as this is often made of three tiers, providing an ombre coloring. These tiers join each other in set-on ruffle effect. Each succeeding one is wider than the one above it. Sometimes ribbon and lace are stitched together, row above row, until the skirt is made. Again, a skirt is made of deep scallops in petal effect, the scallops bound or machine hemstitched, with tulle or lace used to form an underskirt which will provide a straight lower edge.

The skirt or waist-line of such a dress is usually the ornamented part, so let fashion guide you in the selection of a design and allow these instructions to aid you in constructing it in the simplest and most satisfactory manner.

Basque dresses often have bias organdie collar and cuffs with generous bias sashes of organdie, all edges of the organdie finished with a narrow machine hem. Old fashioned corsage bouquets of flowers and lace frequently are used at the center front waist-line. Streamers of ribbon hang to the bottom of the skirt front. Again, when organdie or lace trims the neck and sleeve edges only, narrow velvet ribbon may hang from the center back to the bottom of the dress.

In the dress, Fig. 131, which has capelet sleeves, we see a basque dress with a different air, achieved almost entirely by the addition of the capelets and yoke of the skirt. Frequently voile, georgette or chiffon is used to make such a shoulder cape on frocks of firmer fabric. Sometimes, as shown here, the entire dress is made of the sheer fabric.

In finishing the edges of a dress such as this, use machine hemstitching cut for a picot finish, or a narrow French fold binding, or plan to face all edges with a bias facing, the seams machine stitched, the raw edges turned in and whipped down by hand.

The construction of the dresses shown in Figs. 131 and 132 is not unlike that of Figs. 126 and 130, because a close fitting, light-weight-lining is usually used underneath the blouse to obtain the easy blouse effect. Such dresses are appropriate for dress-up wear for girls, and are less sophisticated in silhouette than the basque dresses, a point that may appeal to conservative mothers.

In developing Fig. 131, use a very limp material, such as challis, soft silk or voile. Stitch the shoulder and skirt seams, put the Trimstitch shirrings in and draw them up to fit. Stitch the sleeve seams and under-arm seams of the waist, and make the skirt and waist joining. Turn the hem in the lower edge of the skirt and stitch it. Use a narrow binding for the neck edge and bottom of the sleeves. Place a band of net or fine lawn under the shirrings at waistline and wrists to hold the shirrings and to give support to the fasteners. If a neck opening is required, make this at the back as shown in Fig. 94, page 35.

The dress shown in Fig. 132 is invariably suitable for a young girl. The ray-like tucks taken on the wrong side of the upper part of the dress ornament it, and at the same time provide needed fulness across the front. The slash belt relieves the monotony of a straight around band and allows of a simple bow that through its very simplicity becomes appropriate.

In developing such a dress, put the tucks in first; then seam the dress, bind or face the neck, put in the sleeves, shirr the top of the skirt, and join it to place. Apply the belt at a becoming point. The belt may be of one thickness of material, the slash finished with a narrow piping and the raw edges caught back with hand stitches.

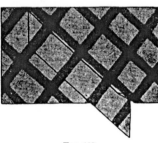

FIG. 127

FIG. 128

FIG. 128. For cording, place cord of the size desired inside a true bias piece cut as for a binding. Bring the raw edges of the bias together and seam them, holding the seam so that the cording foot will crowd the cord in place. When the cord is covered, place it in a seam as desired. Again use the cording foot in stitching the seam finally so that the cord will be wedged close in the seam.

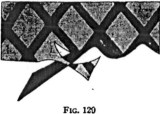

FIG. 129

Festive Frocks. A graduation, party or confirmation frock, considered as a very special frock, is always of importance. The dresses just considered are frequently selected for graduation.

For such an occasion the material may be cream, white or very pale flesh. Neither the fabric nor the design should make the dress definitely different from those worn by the other members of the class. White is generally decided upon and selected by all the girls. Some classes divide themselves into two, three or four groups and select pastel shades—pale jade green for one group, pink for another, corn color for another, lavender for another—using for the dresses exquisite, fast color voile or organdie, which gives a most interesting color effect. This plan needs a teacher's cooperation so that the groups are divided correctly and the dresses selected according to individual becomingness.

For graduation dresses voile, fine batiste, crepe de chine, georgette, organdie and taffeta are appropriate. For party dresses voile, crepe de chine, georgette, organdie and taffeta are desirable. For confirmation dresses voile, swiss, batiste, georgette and crepe de chine fit in best.

If a dress is planned for a special occasion and desired for wear afterward, let the trimming of the dress be of ribbon, tulle or flowers so that it may be taken off and the dress may be used for informal occasions.

Girls who appear before the public, speaking, singing or dancing, should have their dresses designed to be especially suitable for the purpose and of a color and fabric suitable to the stage lighting. Dresses for such occasions usually have a festive, feminine air, and for this reason tulle, lace and taffeta, that make possible bouffant effects, are frequently preferred. Masque costumes are usually of inexpensive material such as paper bunting, imitation silks and gaily printed cottons. When tulle or lace is stitched, use newspaper underneath the seams. This will prevent the material from stretching or tightening. The needle perforates the paper, making it possible to pull it away easily. Crepe paper of good quality may be stitched and gathered on the machine as easily and as satisfactorily as fabric.

FIG. 131

FIG. 130

FIG. 132

Jackets and Coats

FASHION each year gives some new features in coats suitable for school wear. The unlined cloth jacket, shown in Fig. 133, is always fashionable. Its manner of trimming, its color and length are varied each year, but the principle of the coat remains the same. It is sometimes called a sailor coat, again a sport jacket, or a blazer. If it is made longer, to ⅝ or ¾ dress length, then it is simply called a five-eighths coat, or a three-quarters coat. Occasionally the short coat is belted snugly; again, it has a belt sewed to the bottom edge of the coat which allows it to blouse. This is particularly true of blazers.

Suitable materials for such coats are cotton suiting, linen, piqué, broadcloth, or any of the silks similar in weave to the cotton fabrics mentioned. In the woolens, flannel, basket weaves and serges are best. Velvets and velveteens are also appropriate. Sometimes conspicuous checks or stripes are employed. Sometimes military braid or a sleeve insignia is used. Fashion dictates also whether the coat is single or double-breasted, and what the location and the kind of buttons are.

In styling the garment it is important to have the color, fabric and trimming, as well as the construction lines, wholly in keeping with the mode.

Coats such as this may be made all of a length to come to the bottom of the dress. If the fabric is cravinetted it can serve as a real protection for dresses in rainy weather. In such cases the back yoke is usually lined for warmth and additional protection to the shoulders.

In summer a georgette coat on similar lines, made full dress length, is often very practical for wear over dresses of gay colors or prints.

Tailored bathrobes for girls are cut and finished the same as the jacket coat, except that they are made longer, and a tie sash is used with belt straps at the waist-line.

To make such a coat, choose a plain pattern, one with or without dart fulness at the shoulders. If there are darts, put them in first. Patch or welt pockets may be used, as one chooses, one on each side above the bottom of the coat if it is a short coat, such as shown in Fig. 133, the other on the left front above the bust line. The collar and front revers are invariably faced with the fabric of the coat, the edges of these, the hem, bottom of sleeves, and all seams bound with bias binding. If the fabric is very closely woven and does not fray when cut, the seams and edges may be left unfinished or notched throughout.

When jacket coats are worn they are accompanied by a simple dress, or a skirt and blouse. The skirt may be plain or circular, plaited all around, or plaited

FIG. 133

59

partially. The blouse may have a square or boat neck faced or bound, or a tailored collar. It may be with or without sleeves.

Occasionally fashion directs that the blouse be of print and the skirt and jacket of plain material. Bright colors are often used for jacket and skirt costumes for sport wear. For instance, a bright red cloth coat with cream wool skirt and cream silk blouse make a very smart costume. For school a plaid two piece frock with blue or brown predominating, and a blue or brown coat, are appropriate.

A skirt that is plain, especially in the back, and that is to be worn with a coat such as shown in Fig. 133, should, because the jacket will hold the skirt in, have enough fulness at the back to prevent its being shortened in wearing. The placing of the darts, as illustrated in Fig. 134, overcomes any difficulty in this regard. The darts are first pinned in, as shown, then shaped so that there is fulness in the hips while the waist-line is of correct size.

In making coats and skirts such as are considered here, basting, accurate stitching, and progressive pressing are necessary. Press each section before it joins another. An iron should be kept close at hand so that when the garment is finished it will have been pressed throughout, and will need only a final pressing to give an effect of freshness and newness.

Sweater Coats. Sweater coats are often cut of yardage in sweater style, as in Fig. 135. As a rule such materials are expensive and one must measure the length required carefully so that there will be no waste. When tubing is used one usually buys one length for the blouse, plus sleeve length. One tube width serves to cut both sleeves.

Such fabrics are usually designed to require little trimming except to be finished with inconspicuous facings or hems. When a designed fabric is used it is best to buy a plain fabric of similar texture and of slightly darker color to use for trimming bands, as in Fig. 135. These may be cut on the length or the cross. The length is generally preferred, as the opposite grain helps to hold the garment to shape.

In making such a garment, if a knitted fabric is used take care to stretch it slightly in length before cutting to prevent the garment's sagging down when worn. If the fabric curls on the edge and it is difficult to make it stay flat on the table in cutting, use thumb tacks to hold the corners down.

If a crosswise design or stripe is used, as in this case, match the design in the sleeves with that in the blouse. To do this lay the blouse section down and the piece from which you are to cut the sleeves with the design lines even. Place the sleeve pattern on so that the top of the sleeve seam comes parallel with the under-arm seam of the blouse. This will bring the stripes in line all the way around.

In applying facings, stitch them first to the wrong side and then bring them over to make the final

FIG. 134

60

stitching from the right side, thus insuring a true stitching line.

Because such materials fray easily, it is better to have machine worked buttonholes. Mark with basting thread or machine stitching just where you want the buttonholes to come.

Full Length Coats. As a general rule a coat that is used "for best" one year becomes a school coat the next. Therefore, simplicity should be the dominating feature of any coat purchased for girls of school age.

In selecting a fabric for a junior or a junior miss, be sure that when finished it will look as though it were intended for a young girl rather than for a small sized woman. Novelty woolens are usually preferred to plain fabrics, and *colors* rather than *shades*. Navy or soft Dresden blue, reseda green, warm browns and tans, prove better than the adult

Fig. 135

colors of black, gray or bottle green. Novelty woolens, plain serges, and velveteen, because of the possibility of stitching and opportunities for self-trimming, take on a juvenile smartness that is altogether desirable, while striped woolens, velvets and satins appear at once too old.

The coat with epaulet shoulders shown in Fig. 136, developed of soft serge or flannel in blue, with the lining of tan or gray silk, or of autumn brown with a tan lining, is appropriate for the average junior girl. The shoulders, collar line, cuffs, pockets and belt all combine in this design to give a desirable jauntiness. Eliminate the pockets, cuffs and belt, and the coat at once takes on a maturity that is to be avoided in designing coats for girls.

The raglan sleeve coat shown in Fig. 137 is made of heavy novelty coating. The fabric itself is appropriate for juniors in both its design and color. The fabric dominates the design sufficiently to make it

possible to use lines as simple as shown. The coat may have fur collar and cuffs, or welt pockets, or a belt, or it may be developed simply as shown here. If a plain fabric is used, then the addition of these design features should be considered.

In making a coat of heavy fabric, take care in making the seams to press them open wherever possible to avoid overlapping of material, and to cut away any excess bulk at corners, inside hems, or any place that might appear thick. Light weight muslin interlining is used underneath the front facings of Fig. 138. This is allowed to extend a little beyond the facing line so that the break between the facing and the coat will not be too definite.

The collar and cuffs are double. The collar is

Fig. 136 joined with the front facing. The cuffs are added

FIG. 137

to the sleeve edges, the seams pressed open, and stitched as in the right sleeve *a*. The cuffs are then brought back as in the left sleeve *b*. The lining is whipped to this.

If pockets are used, place them beyond the front facing, and put them in and press the coat thoroughly before the lining is put into the coat. The hem is brought up and catstitched to the coat also before the lining goes in.

Lining Coats. In cutting a coat lining there are two differences from the way the coat itself is cut. The first is to place the center back of the coat pattern 1 inch from the fold to allow for a plait at the center back. This provides ease inside the coat and prevents the lining from pulling out when worn. The second is to turn the pattern back on the line of perforations indicated for the facing. The lining should be sewed to the inside edge of the facing, not extend over on it.

When the lining is cut, baste the plait at the center back. Stitch the under-arm and sleeve seams and clip the seam edges to prevent their drawing. Press the plait in and the seams open. Turn the coat wrong side out and baste the sleeve seam of the lining to the sleeve seam of the coat, using strong thread and long, easy stitches so that the lining will be easy on the seam but will be held to position and not twist out of place. When the lining is correctly in place in the sleeves, all seams will be inside.

Turn the raw edge of the lining at the bottom and pin it ready for felling. Bring the top of the sleeve lining up to the armhole seam and baste it to the seam, easing in the fulness so that the fabric grain in the lining comes in the same position as the fabric grain in the sleeve.

Baste the plait in the coat lining to the center back of the coat; then baste the side seams of the lining to the side seams of the coat in the same way as for the sleeves. Bring the front shoulder of the lining up first and baste it to the shoulder seam of the coat; then bring the back shoulder and back neck to position. Fell the armhole of the coat lining down over the sleeve lining and the lining at the center front down over the facing. The lower edge may be finished as explained for the baby coat on page 16, or the lining may be turned up to form a 1-inch tuck at the bottom and slipstitched to the hem of the coat at the top edge of the tuck.

FIG. 138

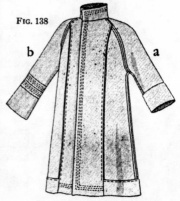

Pajama Costumes

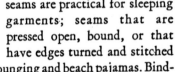

PAJAMAS have become popular with girls of all ages and are particularly practical for sleeping, lounging, and for beach wear.

Sleeping pajamas are usually made of gay or pastel colors and the edges bound with bias binding or finished with narrow facings. Beach pajamas are made in one piece, two pieces, even in three pieces, and of all types of fabrics, especially firm cottons, jerseys, and heavy silk. Lounging pajamas are often made of silk, light-weight woolens, or firm cottons.

The pajama pattern should be bought according to bust size, just the same as a dress pattern, and should be altered for correct length. Pajamas should be loose and easy, and, for practical wear, made entirely by machine so that the seams will be sturdy and in keeping with the fabrics that are suitable for pajamas. French or flat-stitched seams are practical for sleeping garments; seams that are pressed open, bound, or that have edges turned and stitched are preferred for lounging and beach pajamas. Bindings, pipings, or facings are generally chosen for edge finishes. All edges are finished to harmonize.

Gay, bright colors are favored. Pajamas express considerable individuality and allow an expression of personal preference.

Fashion should dictate the finish of pajamas, for edge trimmings and waist-lines, as well as color combinations. Pajamas should be smart, above all, and in perfect accord with the fashion. It is a good idea to see smart pajamas in the better shops and fashion books, then to buy the type of material appropriate for copying those that you like, and then to make them. It will be readily seen how better materials and workmanship will give you a value and thereby repay you for the time and effort required for the making.

FIG. 139A

FIG. 139

Reference Index

Relative Sizes of Needles and Thread

(Class and Variety of Needles Used, 15 x 1)

Sizes of Needles	Classes of Work	Sizes of Cotton, Silk or Linen Thread
9	Georgette, chiffon, light-weight rayon, fine dimity, lawn, batiste and other feather-weight or sheer fabrics. For infants' clothes and for dainty lingerie, also fine lace and all delicate or gossamer fabrics.	100 to 150 Cotton OO & OOO Silk Twist
11	All medium light-weight, summertime fabrics. For children's clothes, dainty house dresses and aprons, glass curtains.	80 to 100 Cotton O Silk Twist
14	Light-weight woolens, firm dress silks and cottons, draperies and fabric furnishings. For smocks and men's fine shirts. For general household sewing; for fine quilting.	60 to 80 Cotton A & B Silk Twist
16	Heavy cretonne, madras, muslin and quilts. For stitching aprons and men's work shirts. For making buttonholes.	40 to 60 Cotton C Silk Twist
18	Bed ticking, awnings, porch furniture covers, boy's duck suits.	30 to 40 Cotton D Silk Twist
19	Heavy weaves of coating, suiting, ticking, sacking, tarpaulin, duck, drilling, canvas. For wash uniforms and bedding supplies for hospitals and hotels.	24 to 30 Cotton E Silk Twist 60 to 80 Linen
21	Bags, Coarse Cloths and heavy Goods.	40 to 60 Linen or very Coarse Cotton

When sending orders for needles be sure to specify the size required.

You will obtain the best stitching results from your sewing machine if it is fitted with a Singer needle.

The Sign of

Singer Service

SINGER
SEWING
MACHINES

Throughout the World

Printed in the United States
55607LVS00004B/274